The Game and Play Leader's Handbook

The Game and Play Leader's Handbook

Facilitating Fun and Positive Interaction

Revised Edition

Bill Michaelis
John M. O'Connell

Venture Publishing, Inc.
State College, Pennsylvania

Production Manager: Richard Yocum
Manuscript Editing: Valerie Fowler, Richard Yocum
Cover Design: Diane K. Bierly

Library of Congress Catalogue Card Number 2003116249
ISBN 1-892132-48-6

Dedications

To Dinah, my best play partner and friend who truly does have an elf in her-self—for encouraging my foolishness and lightening my life with love and laughter.

To my grown "kids" Paige and Jay and their "families"—for your heart and humor.

To Fred T. and Robert G. for your legacy of lunacy.

To all the players and leaders along the path that I've had the privilege of learning from and playing with.

And finally, to my dear friend, coauthor, and teammate JMOC Thanks for your hard work, inspirational ideas, continual amazement and amuse-ment, and that big Irish grin. May we continue to find fun and flow at least into triple overtime of the well-played game.

To TMO, my "boy toy" who keeps inspiring me with his playfulness and cre-ativity. You seem to be a natural at inventing games. Keep them coming. Stay playful, stay happy!

To Susie, my Lady Love, who puts up with an inordinate amount of playfulness and helps me keep my life somewhat in order. Here's to your shy playful little girl and organized big girl. Thanks for all your help.

To all my family members for all the play training we did in those early years. And all the experience I gained in getting "problem children" to play since then. It's been a blast.

Last, to Dr. Willy. Through thick and thin, ups and downs, tears and fears—you've been there for me. You've also been able to bring a good heart and a good laugh. You kept this thing going when I would have probably lost it on my desk. Thanks for your friendship, your courage, your determination and most of all your unrelenting play spirit. Let's do it again next lifetime.

Acknowledgments

A special thank you to Venture Publishing, Inc. (specifically Valerie Fowler, Richard Yocum, and Diane K. Bierly) for a positive professional working relationship with us that respected our expertise and our knowledge of the scope of the subject matter. It was a pleasure.

Thanks to all the folks along the way (you know who you are) who helped transcribe early talking tapes of this book and typed various chapter drafts—most recently, Barbara Enes and Edwin Tse. Thanks for keeping it moving.

And thanks, Geof, for your early and ongoing encouragement...and faith that playmakers are important for the twenty-first century.

Most of all, we want to thank all the members of the New Games Gang. You know who you are (and we know where you live!)—the trainers and the players. You taught us most of what we know and made our lives and work a lot more fun. Thanks for everything.

Contents

Preface

Welcome to the Game

To lead you must be willing to go before.
—Menard Jackson

Hi, and welcome to our book. Or should we say to your book, since you paid for it (presumably). This book is our chance to share with you our experience of play and games leadership.

Exercise 1: Hold your breath and read the next sentence. Safety note: if your eyes begin to go dim, take a breath.

This book is a result of each of us having 25-plus years of play leadership experience, and if you count all the fooling around we did as children then you can add another 20 years each; our experience comes from playing with thousands of people in communities all over the world—people of different cultures and ages and abilities—and finding ways to tap that inner spirit of play in each person and in each group. *Safe. Take a breath.*

Kernel Concepts

There are general concepts and there are kernels of truth, pearls of wisdom so to speak. Kernel concepts may not be as universally important as Peace, Love, and a Good Night's Sleep, but they are important.

Over the years we've discovered three threads relating to play leadership that are woven throughout all the chapters in this book:

1. ***The Play Spirit***. In each of us there is a play spirit. It's an innate part of our higher human nature. As play leaders, it's not only important for us to touch that play spirit in others, but it's doubly important that we keep it alive in ourselves.

2. ***Big Fun***. We've found that in any situation where play is appropriate there are ways to make it more fun, to have a deeper, longer, wider, richer experience sometimes...even a profound one. As play leaders, part of our job is to help people have the best play experience they can have. You could call it *Play Efficiency,* but that might seem like a contradiction in terms. Or you could call it *Optimum Play,* but that sounds very technological. So we just call it *Big Fun*. We like Big Fun. We know you like Big Fun, too.

3. ***The Playful Path***. Life is a journey. We walk along a path and experience a variety of adventures along the way. Depending on which path you choose to walk, you'll have different types of adventures. Kind of like choosing a ride at Disneyland.

Many of us who have touched the Play Spirit deeply in ourselves have chosen to work at helping spark the Play Spirit in others and help them catch some Big Fun. We call that choice to work with play, the Playful Path.

In some ways the Playful Path is a recapitulation of our own lives, our own journeys as players. As children we had important and meaningful play experiences that affected us so strongly that we wanted to keep on playing, for the rest of our lives. As leaders, we want to offer the experience of play and its benefits to others, to kids, to adults, to business executives and prison inmates and senior citizens and anyone we can reach.

Ultimately, the Playful Path is a path of self-development. It's a way to grow and improve ourselves by *serving* others. Sometimes we lose the path, for example a recreation director finds herself shuffling papers all day, or a coach finds himself in a situation where winning is more important than how you play the game. Losing the path is part of the adventure. We know we're back on the path when we're all having fun together.

For us, this book is a way to pull together all of the knowledge, information and tricks of the trade that we've learned from walking the Playful Path in search of Big Fun. It's also for the spirit of play in all of us that never grows old and never stops being alive and excited. This book is an invitation and a ticket. You've got the ticket, so come on along, we're going on an adventure.

Focus on Leadership

> *You can't take anyone anywhere that you're not willing to go yourself.*
>
> —Bob Tannenbaum

Our focus in this book is on leadership. What can you contribute as a leader to *facilitate* play? That is, how can you make it easier for people to play. We'll use *facilitation* frequently in discussing leadership. A leader can't make people play—play has to be voluntary. A leader can't guarantee that people will have Big Fun, that is up to the participants. A leader can work to make the conditions favorable to Big Fun, so that it's as easy as possible for people to play. That is what play facilitation is all about.

The principles and concepts that we'll be talking about are discussed in relation to leading games, but we think that they apply much more broadly as well, to other recreation activities, sports, management, maybe even politics, and life in general. As you read through the book and do the exercises, think about whether you might apply some of the principles you're learning to other areas of your life besides games and play. Maybe you're taking a group on a trip; substitute the word *trip* for *game* and you can now lead the game of camping trip or museum trip. Or maybe you're the President of the United States and you have to figure out how to lead the game of World Peace. Hopefully, the same rules of leadership through facilitation will still apply. Hopefully, you'll also find them useful in whatever leadership roles you happen to take on in your life.

Our Biases

Principle: We all have biases, beliefs that cause us to tend to see things certain ways. The wise leader learns to recognize his or her own biases and account for them.

We'd like to make you aware of a couple of our biases. We believe:

1. ***Play is important.*** We believe play is one of the most important aspects of life.

- We learn from play.

- We grow from play.

- We communicate and interact positively through play.

- Play is not frivolous activity.

- Play is one of the activities that makes us most fully human.

- We have fun when we play, and we need fun to keep us healthy and alive.

2. ***Play works.*** We believe that play has positive consequences in addition to the direct personal ones mentioned here as important. *Play is a very important tool in building community.*

- Play facilitates understanding.

- Play brings people closer together.

- Play transcends barriers.

- Play works as a tool for team building in corporations and neighborhoods and schools and the world.

- Playing well together helps establish the trust and cooperation necessary for a more peaceful world.

- Play allows us to celebrate our differences rather than fight over them.

3. *It has got to be fun.* Yes, amidst all of these beliefs, there is one above all others which we hold near and dear. It has got to be fun. Preferably, Big Fun. Otherwise, why do it? If it is fun, all of the good things listed here will emerge. If it isn't fun, you'll probably never get that far.

A Word to the Wise

Principle: The more you put in, the more you get out.

This is a leader's *handbook.* It's meant to fit in your hand or your pocket or backpack (or small truck if we actually threw in all the sidebar humor we keep thinking of as we write). Most of all this book is meant to be used. It's meant to be referred back to as you plan your programs or when you get into a jam in the middle of a program. More than a theoretical guide to the deep truths of the universe, this book is meant to be a get down and dirty, practical guide to how you can get fun to happen with real people in real situations.

It's your book. At least, it may become your book if you listen to a word from the wise: *Do the Exercises!*

Imagine that Bill and John are like Arnold Schwarzenegger and Sylvester Stallone (of course, in prime shape). We never would use any untoward force with you, nor hurt you in unspeakable ways so you wish you had done the exercises, *but if you don't do the exercises, we're going to know about it.*

We know your type. See, we're a lot like you. We read through all kinds of books with all kinds of exercises. Do we do the exercises? No, of course not! Well, sometimes we do some. But we feel badly about it and we have only ourselves to blame for missing a learning experience. You should *do the exercises:*

- Because they're pretty fun.

- Because you'll probably learn something.

- Because you'll be looking for the answers someday when you're in a jam on a program and you'll be saying to yourself, "Oh, dear Bill and John, why didn't I listen? Why didn't I do the exercises when I had the time?" But it will be too late then.

There are two parts to this book. Our part and your part. Our part is done. We've led hard, difficult lives scratching out nuggets of golden wisdom from the rocky earth of a lifetime of fun and games. Now we're giving all that we've learned to you. (For only the price of this book!)

Now it's up to you. Your part is to *do the exercises,* write in the book, make notes for future reference, add to it, change it, even, Earthball forbid, scratch parts out. Make it your book. Just as in baseball, where the manager keeps "The Book" with all the notes, updated after every inning, on how each pitcher pitched and how each batter batted, this is now your book, to keep your notes on what worked and what didn't.

If you do that you'll keep improving as you walk the Playful Path. By the time you finish this book you'll be a much better leader because you'll be practicing a basic leadership process—*thinking* about what you hope to do, *doing* it (as well as you can, no better, no worse), *reflecting* on what you've done (and how you might do it better)—*thinking, doing, reflecting,* over and over. It's called practice. It's what great leaders do. They practice leadership, just like great martial artists practice their art or great spiritual teachers practice their religion. As leaders continue to practice, they get better, as they get better, they get the opportunity to practice leading more challenging activities. The question sometimes comes up, "How long does it take to get good at this?" The simple answer is, "The rest of your life."

Learning to Lead, Learning to Learn

Principle: Move from unconscious incompetence to unconscious competence.

Learning to lead, like learning almost anything else of significance, is a process. That means it takes a while and there are a number of steps involved. Be prepared, the path may at times be difficult.

You might imagine that learning to have fun while helping others to have fun, would be a fun thing to do. There are plenty of fun times. Then there are times when the learning is not fun, when it's difficult, frustrating, anxiety producing, sad or just plain depressing. At these times you need fortitude and discipline, especially discipline. You need the discipline to keep on going when it would be easier to stop. Most of all you need the discipline to keep on believing in yourself, that you can and will succeed, even when it seems easier not to believe in yourself. Just do it!

There are a couple of predictable patterns to the learning process that we can tell you about, so that as you hit some of the rough spots on the path you won't flip out too badly. First, learning anything is a process of moving from *unconscious incompetence,* to *conscious incompetence,* to *conscious competence,* and finally in some cases to *unconscious competence.*

You may be at any of these stages in the learning process when it comes to play leadership. Where you are is not tremendously important, but it's helpful to know. Once you know where you are, you can proceed to head for where you want to be in an effective way. Being unconsciously incompetent is often a very comfortable place; blissfully ignorant of all there is to know, not knowing what you don't know, it's easy to be content. However, this is also a very weak place. Not knowing something leaves you at the mercy of the universe. It assumes that what you don't know isn't going to be needed and that you aren't going to be competent to provide it. So it's comfortable but not safe. It's a bad place to be.

As you move on to being aware of what you don't know, conscious of your incompetence, you lose your comfort, and if anything, you become painfully aware of how unsafe a situation you are in. This, however, is a very good place, because now you at least know what you have to do. Still you may have some feelings of anxiety, frustration, and so forth. We talked about that previously. If you hang in though, things do start to get better.

As you practice you begin to recognize that with conscious effort, you can be a good leader; that is a consciously competent leader. Once you hit this level, even though you may still be aware of the risks and the difficulties involved in being a decent leader, you have frequent experiences of fun and satisfaction to keep you motivated. So being consciously competent is a nice place to be, and it's reasonably safe.

Sometimes we can become good enough at something, say playing guitar or being a play leader, that we're able to do that thing quite well without even having to think about it very much. In some ways, this is the ideal that we all strive for, the master who glides effortlessly along, always making the right move without ever seeming to work at it. This is unconscious competence. There are times when play leadership can be like that, when it is pure joy to work with a group and it seems like it is happening almost without you having to do too much. A few small moves, a clever comment at just the right time, and the play just takes off.

This is a wonderful stage to be in, and it can also be dangerous. It's easy when you become a good leader to become complacent, to let yourself stop learning and stop practicing the things that helped you to get good. When a good leader becomes complacent, it can be dangerous for everyone.

So be prepared. Watch out for those bogs that make you want to quit as you're learning, and especially for those swamps in which you can get mired after you start to get good.

Another important aspect of the path to be aware of is that it's rarely straight. There are often dips and curves and switchbacks. We seldom find ourselves heading straight and smooth to our goal of being a great leader. It often seems we do too much of this and maybe not enough of that. We are too directive or we are not directive enough.

Recognize that this is part of the process. We're always going to be making corrections to try to keep on course. In the beginning, we may have to make drastic corrections, say to learn safety awareness to keep from getting someone injured. As we improve, hopefully, we stay more on course and the corrections become slighter and smoother, until perhaps we're the only ones that even know a correction was made.

Just remember, making corrections is natural and it's ongoing. Thomas Edison said he learned 362 ways not to make a light bulb before he learned one good way to make a light bulb. Fortunately, he didn't quit making corrections. So hang in there, keep correcting and keep on the path. You will succeed.

Disclaimers

- This is not a games book, although you'll find games in it. Learn to play and lead one game well and you'll soon find that you know all the games you need to know.

- This is not a book on specific games leadership, although you may find us referring to specific situations at certain times. We're more interested and concerned with the rules that apply generally to play leadership with any type of person than with giving recipes for what to do with 42 Tasmanian third graders on rainy days in September or 7 tax lawyers in a computer networked staff meeting. You can figure those things out yourself.

- This is not a book of checklists, although you may find a number of lists in the book. Make your own lists, they can be helpful; but more importantly, get the spirit of play in your guts and heart and head.

- This is not a book on the *theory* of play leadership, although we may mention a few. Mostly we're going to throw out a few cosmic principles and then get down to the nitty gritty practical realities of what works and what you want to put a big red X through and say, "Don't ever do that again!"

This is a book based on our experience. It comes from the heart and the spirit of play. So with that spirit, read it, enjoy it, and *do the exercises!*

Have Big Fun.

Bill and John

Chapter 1

On Playing on Purpose

Play is the exaltation of the possible.
—Martin Buber

One does not stop playing because one grows 'old'...one grows 'old' because one stops playing.
—George Bernard Shaw

The otter is playful, the beaver industrious...which leads the better life?
—Li-tzu

Before passing Go and collecting $200, complete the following exercises:

Visualization. Close your eyes and take a couple of minutes to get in touch with the rhythms of your breathing. Then recall and visualize a wonderful, powerful play experience you had as a kid. It could be something simple or something very involved; it could be organized, unorganized or spontaneous; it doesn't matter. Try to see it clearly in your mind's eye and capture as much of its essence as possible. Stay with it for a while. Then briefly answer the following questions:

1.   What did you visualize? _____

2.   What were some of the qualities and feelings that were associated with it? _____

Fill in the Blanks.

1.   Three things that alert you to the fact that you're playing are:

    _____

    _____

    _____

2.   One of the differences between play and *not play* is:

    _____

Multiple Choice. Circle the best correct answer (or the cutest) to complete the sentence. Play is:

a.   Spelling *pop* backwards with one eye closed

b.   The monkey house at the zoo

c.   Cheating at solitaire

d.   Catching Frisbees on the beach

e.   Eating the filling *first* from an Oreo cookie

f.   A topic that most of the giants of behavioral and social science have written about

g.   Doodling at a corporate board meeting

h.   Making musical sounds with your body

i.   Touch football in the backyard

j.   Play Station

k.   Not trivial

l.   All of the above (at least sometimes)

m.   Making up questions and responses like this

That's right—if you answered *m* you're correct. Special dispensation will be given for those who answered *l*; you'll still be allowed to proceed with this chapter. If you gave a different response you're required to participate in at least three of the activities in the other responses before proceeding (and we're checking!).

Play is indeed all of the above and so much more. We do believe in the power of play (otherwise we wouldn't have written this book) and we believe in the poetic power and profound purpose of players and play leaders like you (say that three times fast).

But what is this thing called *play?* If we asked someone on the street he or she might not be able to give us an academic definition, but he or she could identify some qualities and feelings associated with it. We almost all know play when we see it or feel it. What are some of the qualities that you wrote down in the first two exercises?

A clear definition of play is often slippery and elusive. And in this culture play is still often trivialized ("It's just child's play"), deferred ("Get all your work done first and then you can play"), and/or infused with guilt ("Why are you wasting your time fooling around when you could be doing something more constructive with your life?"). *But play does in fact have profound developmental and health benefits for all of us, children and adults alike.* It's not our purpose to list every definition or every value of play ever described in the literature. Indeed almost all major behavioral and social scientists (e.g., Piaget, Erickson, Bruner, Montague, Freud) have written extensively about the power and purpose of play and we invite you to explore their work in more depth.

Our purpose in this chapter is to highlight a few of the qualities and values of play that clarify our role as play facilitators. We'd also like to illustrate the fact that play occurs across a very wide spectrum of human behaviors and environments, a fact that we believe has profound implications for individual and collective well-being. And last, we'd like to suggest how all this fits with our focus of facilitated play experiences through games.

Some Qualities

Simply put, play is an attitude of lightness, process, transformation, serendipity, open-endedness, creativity, foolishness and *fun.* It can be part of a game or an activity—but not necessarily. It depends on the players, the situation, the setting and *you* as the play facilitator. Play *at its best* is an *attitude* or *spirit* that *communicates* the *freedom* and *joy* of doing what you want to. Go back and look at the multiple choice exercise and you'll see that you have a pretty good sense of when play has disappeared or been subverted. That quality of playfulness is what we're going for as play facilitators. It's bigger and more powerful than any game, any art activity, any special event. It's that transcendent spirit!

Some Values of Play(fulness)

The following are but a few of the potential values of play(fulness) described in the literature. We hope that they serve to illustrate that play is not trivial and that it has profound developmental and health benefits for all of us. It's both "light" and "serious."

- *Complex Learning*. Bruner says that play is "the work of the child" and the primary way that children interact with the world. How did you learn to speak? Probably through playful interaction, and nursery rhymes. How did you learn your colors and numbers: Candyland, finger plays? What else did you playfully learn in those early years?

- *Skill Development*. Did you ever learn to ride a bike or ski or play basketball or paint a picture? All of these skills contributed to your sense of self.

- *Social Learning*. Did you ever play doctor? Did you ever learn to take turns? How did you learn what it was to be a man or a woman (or a human being)? What about competitive and cooperative behaviors? Was at least some of this learning from play and games?

- *Maintaining a Sense of Wonder*. Keeping the "kid" alive in all of us. A sense of childlike innocence. A joy in the hatching of a baby bird and the magic of existence...Growing "young" and maintaining your spiritual, sensual connection with the world.

- *Fantasy, Imagination and Creativity*. No invention ever occurred without the play of the imagination...the turning of the world upside down and inside out, the exploration, the self-expression.

- *An Exercise of Our Deepest Levels of Freedom and Choice*. The open-endedness to do nothing or something or several things to give ourselves pleasure. Our play choices help make us uniquely human. They can help open us up and touch the core of our existence.

- *Self-Esteem*. We know that one of the most important factors in learning is "believing that you can." Play at its best helps create a safe, challenging, win-win nurturing atmosphere where we can reach and stretch and learn and grow and *have fun*. We become empowered.

- *The Ability to Change, to Risk, to Flex, to Adapt, to Roll With the Punches in a Rapidly Changing World*. Play is a joyful process of transformation. If the game isn't working, change the rules (or at least laugh at its absurdity). Play and games are wonderful metaphors for change.

- *A Contribution to Stress Reduction, to Mental and Physical Health, and to a Sense of Balance in Our Lives*. We know that Type A heart-attack prone people have a great deal of difficulty playing around and just "letting go." And we know how good we feel after a good play session!

- *Laughter and Play as Healing Tools*. More and more literature accumulates on the physiological (as well as emotional) benefits of joy in our lives. After a good play or laugh session our systems are flooded with natural pain reducers, tension relievers and mood elevators. What floor are you going to?

• ***High-Tech and High-Touch***. A whole generation of youth has at least been partially educated about technological advances through computer games, by playing. This will continue to happen and provide an opportunity to explore new worlds. But play also provides a much needed opportunity for "high-touch" through environmental education, adventure-risk activities, social games, and hugs. We need both in our rapidly accelerating world.

• ***Problem-Solving Initiative Skills***. By playing around with challenges, environments, and materials, one often discovers unique solutions to problems, new uses for products, and so on.

• ***A Sense of Community and Connection***. Play has the ability to bring us together in more caring, trusting and communicative ways; to connect families, friends, and neighbors. It provides another much needed element of high-touch in our high-tech world. Play has the potential to be a very powerful tool for peace, multicultural understanding, and global well-being because it helps build bridges and break down barriers.

As play facilitators we have the ability to influence the emergence and nurturance of these values.

Some Forms and Contexts

Another way to remind ourselves of the power of play is to remember the multitude of forms and human and environmental contexts in which it occurs. A few modest examples:

• with your cat

• in the moment of a joke or funny thought

• play with equipment

• play with no equipment

• quiet games

• theater play

• mental games

• physically active play

• arts and crafts material play

• media play

• technoplay

• sports

• inside

• outside

- guessing games
- tag games
- board games
- with Jell-O
- with your homework
- while commuting
- sitting in circles
- naked
- with hats
- under the weather
- over mountains
- with lists like this
- ropes courses
- team games
- under water
- in the snow
- in the bathroom
- in the bedroom
- in the air

- in your mind
- at work
- organized
- unorganized
- with your food
- with yourself
- with others
- self-directed play
- at the toll booth
- riding in elevators
- in the dark
- with your housework
- standing in lines
- with uniforms
- with music
- leader-directed/facilitated
- under the covers
- across the sea

We believe that by being open to the variety of play "tools," contexts, and possibilities available to us in life, we increase our capacity for joy in our existence and improve our capabilities of facilitating that for and with others. What matters is the transcendent spirit of playfulness. For example, I know a person who does rock-n-roll dishes with fast, motivating music and when he vacuums he imagines his vacuum cleaner is an alligator eating all the dirt. A little crazy, but definitely more fun, more motivating (and the job gets done). Just think about it. What could we do with play to make our commutes more pleasant, our exercise more motivating, our workplace more happy and team-oriented? How could we keep sports fun for kids and help families find fun together? With all our play tools and a little imagination, the possibilities are endless. But this book is not. So we're going to focus on facilitated, *leader-directed play* using primarily games as our structure for joyful human interaction. It is our hope, however, that the principles, techniques, and spirit that we share in this book will have the widest possible applications.

Elements of the Play Experience

In utilizing games to facilitate the play experience, we've found five elements usually present. These elements provide a useful framework for understanding the play that we'll be referring to throughout this book:

1. *The Players*. These are the people who participate in the game. Does a tree that falls in the forest make any noise? Does a game that doesn't have any players really have play? We're pretty sure that it doesn't.

2. *The Games*. We're using the word *game* in the broadest sense. It's the structure, the activity, and the set of interactions that we happen to agree upon as we play. If playfulness is the spirit or life blood, this is the bones.

3. *The Setting*. The setting is the physical environment in which the game takes place. Is the surface hard or soft, rough or smooth? Is it on land, in the water, or in the air? Is there grass, are there sprinkler heads, are there gopher holes? Are there cement pillars in the middle of the gym?

4. *The Situation*. The situation is the mental-emotional environment in which the game takes place. Is it part of a birthday party or a company picnic? Is it a learning situation in a classroom? Is it an executive team-building situation in a Fortune 500 boardroom?

5. *The Leaders*. That is you. That is us. That is whoever happens to be making a contribution to making the game work. There is a role and a contribution that is made by the leader in terms of organizing, adding order, and/or guiding the open-endedness of play into a structure which helps to perpetuate its spirit and often helps make it easier to find. To facilitate means to make easier.

All five of these elements interact with each other and need to be taken into account if the facilitation of playfulness is to occur.

Summary

- Playfulness is primarily an attitude, a spirit, and a communication system.

- Play has profound developmental and health values for all of us.

- Play occurs in many forms and contexts providing potential powerful possibilities.

- Facilitated play experiences using games contain five elements: the Players, the Game, the Setting, the Situation, and the Leader.

The goal of the leader is to facilitate that spirit of playfulness that will allow healthy growth and development for all participants. The rest of this book will suggest principles and techniques that will help you do it.

Play on...

Chapter 2

The Fundamentals of Play Leadership

It don't mean a thing if it ain't got that swing.
—Duke Ellington

Be careful...you could put your eye out with that.
—Every parent

The *Fun*damentals are enthusiasm and safety! If you forget everything else in this entire book, remember that the most important factors in play leadership and facilitation are *enthusiasm* and *safety consciousness.*

Enthusiasm and Safety

A leader is one who is willing to "go before"—to show the way. A facilitator "eases the passage" for others. By showing your enthusiasm, you go before, and make yourself a leader. Your enthusiasm eases the passage of other players, encouraging their enthusiasm, and thereby making you a facilitator.

Unbridled enthusiasm, however, is not enough. Once the enthusiasm of all players is activated, it's necessary to channel that enthusiasm, so that the activity can be played out in a safe way. As a leader, you hold the bottom-line responsibility for the safety of all participants. If you can bring forth your own enthusiasm and use it to generate enthusiasm in others, and make sure that amidst all the enthusiasm the game is still played safely, then you'll go a long way toward being a great leader.

Another aspect of facilitative leadership is the ability to empower others. As we discuss safety and enthusiasm we'll see that one of the key ways a leader promotes those qualities in a play situation is through empowering the players. Empowerment becomes a *next*damental, a basic method for accomplishing the *fun*damentals.

In this chapter we'll discuss enthusiasm, safety, and empowerment and how to develop these qualities in a play group. Let's start at the beginning with enthusiasm.

Enthusiasm

Ultimately, all we have to give is ourselves. We can best lead other people in play by sharing our own enthusiasm. When each and every one of us extends our own individual spirit and energy, it serves to reinforce itself and reflects back on all the members of the group. This creates a rising spiral of playfulness, caring, spontaneity, and creativity.

Showing our enthusiasm really is sharing ourselves. Enthusiasm is derived from the Greek words *en theos,* meaning "the spirit of god" (*theos*) "within" (*en*). The play spirit that is within us is the spark that can ignite the play spirit in the people we work with. Your enthusiasm provides the energy that gets the play spirit moving in others. In Europe, play leaders are often referred to as "animators," the ones who give animation, movement, and life to players and activities. The way to give that spirit of life to others is through showing your own enthusiasm.

One way to clearly see how important your enthusiasm is, is to look at what it would be like without it. Suppose you went before a group of people and said, "Hey folks, I've got this game you might want to play. I'm not that crazy about it myself. I'm not even sure I would play it if I weren't the leader but it's OK, so maybe you'd like to try it anyway?"

By the time you finished speaking most of your players would have left to do their chores. Cleaning their rooms and doing their homework would have seemed exciting in comparison.

You'll probably get a much better response by choosing an activity that you're genuinely excited about and being able to say to the group, "Hey everybody, I've got a great game I want to show you. It's really fun."

Enthusiasm is the *personal* spirit you as a leader and facilitator contribute to the play experience. It's important to remember that each person's way of expressing his or her enthusiasm is a reflection of his or her personal style. Some people may be loud and boisterous, others may be quiet with a sparkle of subtle humor. What is most important about enthusiasm is that it be genuine; it should come from the heart and soul. When it does, then we can reach the heart and soul of others.

So how do we do that? As we play and show our excitement about a game, a number of things happen. We begin to send out play signals—our smiles, laughs, posture, and movement, as well as our words, communicate a message to the other players that this is fun and that they, too, can enjoy the game. Furthermore, our enthusiasm and energy give permission to and provide a model for players to do the same.

What may start out as a little joke or play on words on your part, can be picked up by others in the group who add to the joke and pass it on until it becomes a running gag. Microplaylets that the whole group creates together (and return to again and again) are a way of building group identity and maintaining group enthusiasm.

There are techniques we use to draw out the enthusiasm of players within a group and to encourage a collective "group enthusiasm." Many of these techniques, sometimes referred to as "cheap tricks," involve encouraging the kinds of behaviors that people who are enthusiastic about something do naturally—like cheering, singing, getting close together, participating actively and moving energetically. Getting people involved in these types of actions helps to prime the pump, so to speak, until the natural enthusiasm of play takes over.

It's kind of like jump-starting a car; you have to push the car a bit to provide the energy for the car to start running on its own. We've included a few cheap tricks you can use to jump-start a group's enthusiasm (see page 12). They can also be used to develop a few ideas of your own.

One thing we can say about enthusiasm is, "What goes around, comes around." Or we could say, "What comes around, goes around." Either way, the enthusiasm you express as a leader will come back to you many fold from the players. Maybe someone in the group will pull off some outrageous maneuver that will fire you up, just at the point that you're starting to drag. Or maybe when you think you've given all you have to give, the one person in the group who never cracks a smile, will suddenly come out with a joke or a great play or a big grin and help you rekindle your play spirit. That is the kind of payback your enthusiasm deserves.

Enthusiasm is a big part of fun. What tends to take the fun right out of enthusiasm is hurt. When someone gets hurt it is no fun for him or her or the rest of the group. So to keep the fun in the game we have to focus on the other *fun*damental of leadership, *safety*.

Safety

Safety is the *sine qua non* of play leadership. Without it there is nothing. By definition, play is a state of being in which a person feels safe enough to open up, to relax, and to take things lightly. If players feel they are in constant danger of being hurt, they may do lots of things, but it probably won't be play.

There are two main aspects of safety, *physical safety* and *psychological* or *emotional safety*. Physical safety is knowing that you are not likely to hurt your body. Emotional safety is feeling that you're not going to hurt your heart and soul. In other words, you're not likely to have your feelings hurt. Both types of safety allow you to go to your own limits without having to spend a significant part of your energy worrying that you're going to get physically damaged or that someone will make fun of you, put you down or reject you.

Every game has safety factors to be considered, be it a fast moving tag game or a sit down word game. A leader needs to develop safety consciousness to anticipate potential hazards in a particular play situation, including

Seven Cheap Tricks to Spark Enthusiasm

1. Do something unusual, playful or intriguing, like using an exclamation point instead of a period!

2. Tell a good joke.

3. Tell a bad joke.

4. Huggle up. When it's time to explain the rules, instead of having everyone just stand around, have them pull close together and put their arms around each other. Explain, "In football the teams have huddles, here we have huggles." The play on words becomes a microgame that generates a few laughs and starts players yelling for everyone to "huggle up" when they want to pull the group together. (Be careful, you may not want to try this early on if your group is composed of juvenile delinquent gang members or IBM executives in three-piece suits. Then again if you can pull it off with these groups you're probably far along on the road to enthusiasm.)

5. Team Names. Have the group make a name for itself, anything from the inspiring to the ludicrous. Whether it's a terrifying totem striking fear into the heart of one's opponents, like the Michigan Wolverines (John's *alma mater*) or a spoof on terrifying totems, like the Santa Cruz Banana Slugs (Bill's spiritual home), making up their own name empowers group members and gives them a sense of ownership and identity.

6. Team Cheers. These are great ways to translate the team name into quick energizers to spark enthusiasm. By letting the group members make up their own cheers, with help as needed from you, you can encourage this team-building activity. It can also tap into people's spontaneity and creativity, getting them mentally and emotionally enthusiastic.

7. Standing Ovation. Make an agreement that at any time during the play session, any player can call a time-out and say, "I want a standing ovation!" Whenever this happens, the rest of the group members will stop and begin clapping and screaming the way they would at the end of a concert by their favorite performer or a come-from-behind, last second win by their favorite team. The person who requested the Standing *O* just stands there and basks in the applause. Oftentimes the requester will say he or she deserves a Standing *O* for a specific reason, but it's perfectly all right to say, "I just want one for being me!" Besides building enthusiasm, the Standing *O* is a great way to welcome new members to a team, show acceptance and boost everybody's sense of self-esteem.

the setting, the game and the particular players involved. Once a leader is aware of potential hazards, the next step is to work with the group to manage those hazards and to protect the players.

We're not saying that as a play leader your job is to eliminate risk and challenge from games. Risk and challenge are inherent elements of games and also part of what makes them fun. Our role as "safety engineers" is to create a play environment which minimizes the possibilities of physical injury and maximizes the potential for each player to come away with a feeling of fun, acceptance, and self-esteem.

Physical safety is an obvious consideration in any active game. What is the setting? Is it safe for the level of action that you might expect with the group playing? For example, you wouldn't play tackle football on an asphalt surface. (Well maybe if you grew up in Hell's Kitchen like Bill did. Or was it Hell's Dining Room?) If you plan to play an active running game, you check the playing area for potholes and sprinkler heads. You might have a nice smooth field to play on, but the grass has just been watered. Serious safety hazard. The first step, and probably the easiest one in safety, is to check the environment, but that is just the beginning.

Eliminating obstacles and other hazards, creating appropriate cushioning, or moving to a safer location are all good starts toward creating safety, but we also have to look at other factors, including the players, the structure of the game itself, the situation (meaning the circumstances in which the game is being played), and last but not least our leadership of the game. The chart presented here provides a framework for helping you analyze a game to anticipate potential safety hazards. Using the chart on page 14, think about the common games listed and what safety considerations might come up in playing them. Try to get past the obvious answers and think of some of the more subtle hazards you might encounter.

Part of the leadership game is to use your creativity in anticipating safety problems and coming up with exciting ways to solve those problems without giving up the challenge of the game. For example:

- What if you have one or two children who are a lot slower than the rest and can never catch anyone in Duck, Duck, Goose. Instead of having them run out of gas and quit or end up in the "mush pot" every time, why not restructure the rules so that if someone has not escaped by his or her third turn he or she gets to pick someone to run for him or her. Or maybe you have a better way?

- Many people are coming up with creative variations in Dodge Ball that allow players to recycle back in after they have been hit out. This allows the game to go on longer and allows players who need the practice to get more playing time. Many play leaders are also

---

Anticipate Potential Hazards

	Physical Safety	Emotional Safety
Players	_____	_____
Game Structure	_____	_____
Situation	_____	_____
Setting	_____	_____

Games:	Duck, Duck, Goose	Who's the Boss?
	Choosing teams	Dodge Ball
	Swat Tag	Boggle
	Octopus	*GHOST*

---

making use of foam balls rather than inflated rubber ones, recognizing that foam balls make the game safer physically and psychologically for the players.

- In the traditional Who's the Boss? one person starts a motion that all the other players follow. At the same time a guesser in the middle tries to figure out who "the Boss" is who started the motion. By having two people or more take the role of guesser instead of one, the added support makes the game safer emotionally for the guessers, introduces an element of teamwork to the guessing, and makes the game more challenging for the rest of the group. You can also increase the safety level for the guessers by allowing them to choose whether they want to guess from standing inside or outside the circle. Those that want more of a challenge can stand in the middle and those who want an easier challenge can stand on the outside.

- In games requiring two equal teams, try picking teams by having each person find a partner of about the same ability. Then have one partner go to team A and the other go to team B. You've just eliminated the emotional pain of being the last one picked and at the same time created even, balanced teams.

In looking at these examples, what is important is to see that there are many aspects to safety and that a little creativity can eliminate many of the pitfalls that otherwise might reduce the fun level of the game. A simple way to stretch your own creativity and safety awareness is to empower the group to identify safety hazards and come up with creative ways around them. As the saying goes, "Two heads are better than one." Likewise five or ten heads are better than one at coming up with ideas for how to deal with them.

You can begin to empower the group to encourage safety just by asking the members, "What do you think the safety factors are in this game?" You can then add in any factors that they might miss. You'll probably find that players are much more responsible about observing safety rules when they have participated in generating them themselves.

Another way to empower the group and to build the members' safety awareness is to call a safety time-out as soon as you see some action take place that may be unsafe. Without blaming the players involved, ask the group members how the actions might create a safety problem and what they think could be done differently. When a group starts to own the responsibility for its own safety, its members start to play more safely.

An example of this is the Ripple Stop Technique. We explain to the players, particularly in a competitive physical game, say a wrestling game, that if at any time anyone perceives that anyone in the game is in danger, he or she is to yell "Stop!" as loudly as he or she can. Whenever anyone hears the word "Stop!" he or she is to stop immediately and also yell "Stop!" The ripple effect this word-of-mouth alert creates can bring a group of dozens of people to a screeching halt within a couple seconds. Because they are in charge of it, and agree to abide by it before the game begins, players almost universally are impeccable in observing and honoring such safety rules.

Be aware that what is safe with one group may not always be safe with another. You may be able to play a game like Hug Tag with third graders but find out that teenagers are mortified by the perceived "childishness" of the game. Also, what is not safe with a group at one point in a play session may become safe within the same group at a later stage of the session or vice versa. You may find that once people have gotten more playful and the emotional safety level of the group has risen, everyone in the group thinks hugging is a terrific idea for a game. On the other hand you may find that an active game which was perfectly safe early in the play session becomes dangerous later on; the situation has changed, the players are now tired.

Game selection, sequencing, anticipation, planning, and empowerment all become tools for managing safety. It is a little like being a raft guide on a whitewater river. You anticipate the dangers in the rapids and plan your strategy, you plan which paddle strokes to use and in what order, and you ask everyone in the boat to look out for the rocks and to help with the steering. Then you get to the rapids and the water is never exactly as you expected and

you all paddle like crazy and somehow you make it through safely. When we all pull together for safety we usually make it through.

In creating the kind of atmosphere in which people pull together, we need to apply the concept of discipline. Discipline is a necessary aspect of leadership and facilitation because one person, or a small number of people, getting out of line may affect the safety of another player or of the whole group. One player may be playing unconsciously or unnecessarily rough. A small group may be making snide remarks about someone else or about everyone else. Instead of identifying the offending parties in front of the group, which will make them feel put down and force them to get resentful or escalate the level of their misbehavior, you can talk to them personally and informally while the rest of the group is playing. By talking to them privately you make it emotionally safe for them to change their behavior without being embarrassed in front of the group.

The basic principle of safety leadership is to use all your resources. Use modeling, demonstrations, examples, verbal reminders, adaptations of the game, and fine tuning of the rules to maintain a high safety level in the game. You may be leading a parachute game where participants run under the chute and trade places when the chute is lifted in the air. You may explain that players need to watch out to avoid collisions under the middle of the chute. Then you may need to demonstrate how easily people can run into each other and how to dodge to avoid collisions. Before you get started you'll probably ask the group members to take a pledge to play safely and after you get going you'll still have to coach several players individually on the art of playing conscientiously. You'll probably have to point out several near misses to the group members and remind them at least once of their safety pledge. At some point you may even adapt the game by adding a few rules such as walking in slow motion while the chute lifters try to keep the chute in the air as long as possible, rather than trying to capture several people underneath.

By the end of the game you'll have used every trick in this book and a bunch more you made up on the spot. And your reward? A couple of kids saying, "Hey, dude, that was a cool game and nobody got wiped out either."

Your safety consciousness allows for freedom, which is maybe *the* essential element of play. It allows players the freedom to be themselves fully, to pass beyond the rules of everyday existence, to laugh and be uninhibited, expressive and spontaneous, to give their best efforts physically, emotionally and intellectually. If you have to worry whether you might look foolish, or be laughed at, if you have to worry whether you might be hurt, you won't have the freedom to play "all out." It is that openness and sense of freedom that allows us to stretch and grow and enjoy the full range of being ourselves. Safety really provides us with the opportunity to freely share our enthusiasm.

What It Is All About

There is an old story that really tells it like it is about enthusiasm and safety. The story goes that the difference between contribution and commitment is that when you have bacon and eggs for breakfast, the chicken makes a *contribution,* but the pig makes a *commitment.*

The bacon and eggs are both an important part of breakfast. (Unless you're a vegetarian, in which case substitute tofu: "The soybeans make a *commitment!*") Likewise, enthusiasm and safety are both important for our enjoyment of play.

Enthusiasm is the personal contribution that each of us makes as a play leader to an enjoyable play experience for our group. Safety is a commitment we all have to make as facilitators to ease the passage of players into the full freedom of enthusiastic play.

So remember, if you forget everything else, don't forget to remember the *fun*damentals _____ and _____ .

> *If you can keep your head when all about you are losing theirs and blaming it on you....you'll be a Man my son!* [or a Woman my daughter...and a Leader.]
>
> —Rudyard Kipling (with apologies)

Chapter 3

Getting It Going

Can't start a fire without a spark.

—Bruce Springsteen

A journey of a thousand miles starts with a single step.

—Anonymous

Now that you know the *fun*damentals, we really ought to get on with it! Leading a game actually involves only three things: a beginning, a middle, and an ending. Any questions? Like a well-delivered speech or well-written novel, well-developed play needs to get off to a rousing start, needs some solid content in the middle, and needs to close well. That is what the next three chapters will be about: How you can lead a game or a series of games as part of a small or large play event.

Basic Concepts

Before taking you through the operational steps of getting a game going, we'd like to acquaint you with a few basic concepts related to play leadership.

The Play Community

One of the primary goals of a play leader is to establish a sense of a caring community. That is, whether we're playing cooperatively and/or competitively we've agreed that we're playing *together* and we're committed to try our best to *play well together* (and to do whatever it takes to accomplish that). Why? Because mostly we like playing for the fun of it and we like playing with each other because we support each other in our pursuit of fun. An elf and games designer named Bernie De Koven once wrote a whole book about this called *The Well-Played Game*. The point is, if we can help establish that "caring play community," there is no telling what kind of growth, surprises, and fun will follow. As leaders there are several things we can do initially to help build that community:

Emphasize Teamwork and Share the Power. Get your players involved in making suggestions for rules, helping with equipment, and demonstrations, and sharing responsibility for safety. The more you do this, the more ownership they will feel of the game. Practice using questioning strategies (e.g., What do *you guys* think? What might make it a better game?).

Emphasize Play as Communication and Communication as Facilitating Playfulness. The greatest percentage of human communication is nonverbal. A smile, a kazoo, a red clown nose, or a funny T-shirt goes a long way toward saying, "Let's play!" It might just be your tone of voice. Another way that you as a leader can facilitate playfulness is to think about and pay attention to all the ways that you can give people "permission" to be playful. That is, letting them know in one way or another (verbally, nonverbally, or by your modeling) it's OK not to be perfect, it's good enough to give it your best shot, big people can play too, and it's OK to be expressive and/or publicly foolish.

Emphasize Involvement and Participation. Fun activities, whether they are competitive and/or cooperative most often need some level of challenge. So try to get folks hooked in mentally, physically, and expressively, but also procedurally (e.g., asking them, emphasizing teamwork). Challenge them to stretch themselves a bit at *some* level. Also emphasize activities that will get everyone involved without a lot of standing around or waiting in lines. Choose or modify games that allow people access to them and don't screen them out because they are not fast enough, or flexible enough, or athletic enough. Choose games that the very widest range of the population can play, whether they are athletic or just have athlete's foot. Providing access to your activities also implies creating the "permission" for egress. That is, anyone at any time should feel free to leave your game if it is not working for him or her or if he or she is not in the right mood. The right to play includes the right not to play and sometimes you have to tell people that. And believe it or not, that freedom helps strengthen the play community.

The last concept related to participation and involvement is *integration*. Play at its best helps to break down barriers and build bridges between people, whether old or young, able-bodied or disabled, Black or White. The playground becomes the common ground where we can laugh together, be challenged together, and win together in the broadest sense.

Attention to all of these factors—teamwork, sharing power, communication, involvement, participation, access, egress and integration—goes a long way to help establish the *play* community. You as a leader can make that happen.

Facilitation Versus Arbitrary Authority

The second major concept we want to emphasize before getting at the operational steps leading a game is *facilitation*. Our whole approach to leadership is that of facilitation or "making things easy" for the people to play (that is what the word actually means) versus commanding them, or having a know-it-all attitude. Your power doesn't come from the fact that you're wearing a black-and-white striped T-shirt and have a whistle around your neck. Your power as a leader comes from the relationships that you establish with your players and from your ongoing trust and confidence in yourself to take risks, to learn from your mistakes, to model foolishness, and to put yourself on the line. That doesn't mean that you won't have to exert higher levels of visibility and authority in some instances (e.g., dangerous situations) but it does mean that your real effectiveness comes from the trust and communication you establish in the play community.

Two last thoughts to keep in mind:

The fun begins with you. What is your own personal playfulness about and how do you communicate it?

You can't take anyone anywhere you're not willing to go yourself. If you want people to risk or be expressive or try or be crazy or "whatever," you've got to be willing to model it, and to express it yourself. So let's get on with it!

A Short Quiz

True or false: Two of the four Ps that are most critical to strong play leadership are *peanut butter* and *pasta*.

If you answered true to this question you are correct (at least for Bill and John). These foods have made us the energetic and enthusiastic leaders that we are today. You need not proceed any further with this book, as you already know our big secret. However, if you answered false, you may proceed because you knew that pasta and peanut butter were not among the Ps that we were going to talk about (either that, or you cheated and skipped a few lines ahead in this book). People who answered true do have the option of changing their answer and proceeding.

The Four Ps of Getting a Game Going: Purpose, Planning, Preparation, and Presentation

Purpose

If you take the time to think through the purpose of your game or play session you'll go a long way toward assuring its success. After all, you want it to be good, to be fun, and to be successful—right? Of course! So although in the beginning it may seem a little overanalytical or time-consuming, we can guarantee you that being clear about your purpose (What do I want to have happen?) and about the group's purpose (What do the players want?) will be the foundation of all of your other activities. For example, do you want them (a) to get to know each other, (b) to be energized, (c) to get some exercise, (d) to develop a sense of teamwork or groupness, (e) to explore and develop more expressiveness and/or communication, (f) to release pent-up tension, and (g) to learn each other's names? What do they want? Or maybe you're playing strictly for the fun of it. So your purpose is *Big Fun for all* (of course, this should probably be the overriding purpose). At the tail end of your game or play session you'll want to do an evaluation of all aspects of your leadership, but the most important question you'll ask yourself is, "Did I adequately fulfill my purpose?" If you don't know what it was, then you can't answer that question (and ultimately learn to improve for the next time). So get into the habit of asking the big question first. With experience you'll be able to answer it (analytically and intuitively) in less and less time. And the time invested in your other steps will shrink also.

Planning

Now that you've thought about the overriding purpose(s) of your game(s) you are ready for the planning stage. What else do you need to know to help you in your decision making and play activity choice? What do you want to play and how do you get there? To sensitively answer these questions it's important *to review and expand on your understanding of the five elements of the play experience* that were introduced in Chapter 1, *On Playing on Purpose*. They are the players, the situation, the setting, the game, and the leader (you).

The Players

- What are their developmental and other needs?

- What are their abilities, likes, preferences, interests?

- What is the size and mix of the group (male/female, boss/worker, older/younger)?

- Are there any "lightning rods" (energetic overt players) in the group?

- What are the "play signals" and/or cultural expectations of the group?

- Are there any popular culture interests or values in the group?

While it's not the purpose of this book to list all of the needs and interests of every group that walked the earth (and besides it would be virtually impossible) we must strongly emphasize that *games are to serve the player,* so you must make your best attempt to be as familiar with your players as possible.

New Games

Our philosophy is that games are a flexible vehicle to create a positive emotional experience for folks, not an arbitrary structure that demands conformity. There are several good references in Chapter 12, *Resources, Connections, and Beyond* that can help you with basic developmental needs across the life span. It's clear that planning games for kindergartners is different from planning a play session for Wells Fargo Bank managers. Having an initial game that is overtly expressive and silly might be just the ticket for a group of five-year-olds but might sabotage your entire play session with the bankers. Likewise, choosing a game with a high challenge and complexity level might be just the ticket for Wells Fargo but would do nothing but create chaos, confusion and a sense of failure for the "munchkins." Knowing your people can make all the difference in the world. If you've got a hotshot player in your group, you can enlist him or her to help demonstrate. That person's energy and enthusiasm will be synergistic. One other example: we invited a bunch of teens to play a team ball-tag game called Monarch where the monarchs had to capture all the peasants by hitting them with Nerf balls. It didn't work. They didn't want to play. However, the movie *Ghostbusters* was a hot hit during the time. The next day we invited a different set of teenagers to play the same game. Only this time we called it Ghostbusters where the ghostbusters had to capture all the ghosts. Voilà! An instant hit! Why? Because we paid better attention to our player's needs, likes, dislikes, and cultural interests. Same game. Different name. Different fantasy. Different results.

The Situation

The situation is the *context* in which you are playing. What is going on? What is the surrounding emotional and activity environment the players are immersed in? What is happening before and after your game session? Is it required? Is it self-chosen? Is it part of a larger event? It's clear that kids in a mandatory gym class is a different situation from a drop-in after-school program. And games at a potluck church supper will likely be different than a required corporate team-building session for a company that has just experienced layoffs. Always try to ascertain to the best of your abilities what context you'll be operating within and be sensitive to its implications. Use questioning strategies with your contact to help you (e.g., Tell me about the group. How long have they been together? Have they done activities before? Like what? What things did they like?).

The Setting

The setting is the physical environment in which you'll be playing. Knowing what it is will help you plan effectively. Never assume anything. Your host may have never led a game in his or her life nor be able to perceive your needs within the environment. Always ask and try to see the setting ahead of time if possible:

- How large is it (e.g., square footage)? What shape is it (e.g., square, rectangular)?

- Is it a hard or soft surface, blacktop, or grass?

- Is it clean and playable? Is there glass, dog droppings, gopher holes, or sprinkler heads?

- Do you have full access to it (is it reserved?) or will there be other groups using it? Doing what? Archery?

- Are there moveable chairs in the indoor space? Are there rugs?

- What is the access–transition time from inside to outside?

- Is there dew on the grass in the morning? Did they stop watering the lawn one or two days before you arrived?

- Can the area be secured?

Knowing your setting will help you plan effectively and flexibly.

The Game

Games are tools that serve people. They are fun tools that stimulate certain types of interaction and levels of energy. *Know your tools* and experiment with them individually and in combination with other tools.

- What level of energy do they require? What level of energy do they create: high, medium, or low?

- Are they competitive or cooperative? What is the level of challenge?

- What is the level of expressiveness required by the group or by the individual? (Charades, for example, requires high individual expressiveness which might be scary or uncomfortable for some folks without enough lead up.)

- What mood do they convey: aggressive? quiet? loving?

Having a sense of what your games "do" (or might convey) will allow you to select from your menu individually or in combination to meet the requirements of the group, the situation, and the setting.

The Leader (You)

You, the leader, are what this book is about. You're the initial catalyst. You want to set the "game activity" and set up for success so you need to ask yourself a few questions:

- Do you have the confidence, experience and support to lead the game or series of play activities?

- Is your play activity pretty simple or very complex? Is it tightly timed with little room for error? Have you led this activity before or is this the first time?

- How much is riding on "successful" performance versus improvisation (flexibility in midstream)? What are the trade-offs?

Set it up for success, but keep taking those steadily calculated risks. Try some games that you're not exactly sure of, but maybe not a complex game like Capture the Flag (at least not initially). Of course with each group, each activity, each experience you'll gain valuable knowledge (game and play knowledge, people knowledge, and self-confidence). Be realistic about your abilities and remember that developing into and being a good play leader is a process. Leave yourself open for surprise. Review the five elements of the play experience each time you plan. It will take less time and become more second nature, with some events requiring concentrated thought and analysis and others just moments to conceive.

A Few Final Thoughts About Planning

Overplan With Flexibility. Amazingly, you might have anticipated 30 people showing up for your game and only six arrived, or they dribble in, in twos and threes, over the course of the first half hour. If you only planned activities that require 30 people, you'll be in trouble and those six folks won't have the benefit of your wonderfulness. If you had a flexible plan that allowed you to change gears due to unanticipated circumstances, you could carry on in great fashion. If you need four or five games for a half hour, plan six or seven.

Have a Few Fail-Safe Games in Your Hip Pocket. These are games that you know almost always work with any group under any circumstances. If all else fails, these may be just the ticket to get things back on track. We'll say more about what we think are some fail-safe games later in this book.

Plan With a MAPP (Maximum Activity Per Player). If you pick games where everyone is active (where there is little standing around or waiting in lines), you've gone a long way toward choosing a successful game. When everyone is active, you're using your time more effectively in a *developmental* way (more movement practice, more social interaction, more exercise, more creativity and self-expression) and you'll have vastly decreased your discipline problems. When folks are involved and active that helps to motivate them in a positive way and they don't need to "act out" or seek attention in negative ways. Even if one of the kids' favorite games is Kickball (with a lot of standing around), find a way to modify it so more folks are involved (there are several ways).

Give Yourself and the Players Enough Time to Be in the Moment, and to Flex if Necessary. As you plan, try not to jam too many games into your time slot or be so agenda-oriented that you can't enjoy the freedom of the playful moment. Suppose people are really enjoying the first game that you introduced and are being playful and creative. Go with it!

Preparation

The preparation stage involves gathering, testing and setup.

Gathering

- What kind and amount of equipment, materials and boundaries do we need?

- Do we need signs that identify the area or "pinnies" to help identify the different teams?

- Suppose more folks show up than we anticipated?

- What kind of help can we gather? Can we get some assistants and volunteers, some folks to help demonstrate or help to set up? How can we use the players to help us?

- What other physical resources do we need: whistles? bullhorns? lime Jell-O?

- Gather information. This takes us back a bit to our planning stage when we emphasized asking elaborate response questions of our game activity site host. Ask for as many specifics as you can get (without being a pain in the butt) about the players interests, the group's background, the physical space, if there is shade or a source of drinking water, etc. And if possible, *see the area ahead of time.*

- Gather your "hip pocket" list. This is your flexibly overplanned script that you'll carry with you that will detail the order, options, potential timing of your activities, and any other buzzwords that will help you remember key points. You should always know your game by heart and be willing and able to improvise, but this is your "anchor."

Testing

This involves practicing your game. Hopefully, some of your friends or family will help with "live practice" prior to your "formal" presentation, but at the very least practice saying the words (even to a mirror if that helps). Remember a good game or play presentation is like a fun speech. Work on confidence and eye contact and ways of communicating your playfulness. If you do practice (even if its only mental rehearsal), you'll be able to anticipate difficulties and devise creative counter solutions. If, after you've explained the game to your friends and family, they give you that blank "you've got to be kidding" look, you know there is something you have to tighten up. Although it might sound negative to anticipate the "worst case scenario" for your game, it will keep you on you toes: What if no one gets tagged? What if the chaser can't catch the chasee? What if the guesser can't guess who is it?

Setup

The setup is how you want the facility and equipment arranged to maximize your playful purpose. Try to send your host a diagram ahead of time detailing how you'd like things set up (e.g., chairs around the periphery, a big open space in the middle, enough mats to sit on, and processing charts on the wall). At the very least, get there early enough to set up the room (or field) and boundaries, remove safety hazards and lay out and group equipment for easy access. And do any other preparation that you'll need to smoothly greet your players and transition into your play session without any logistics worries (e.g., have nametags ready, decorate the room, and have a welcome sign). We'll say more about setup in Chapter 7, *Events or the Big Game*.

Presentation

Question: Gee, Bill and John, it sure is taking a long time to get this game going. Will I still be alive by time this chapter is over?
Answer: Choose one or more:

   a. Rome wasn't built in a day.

   b. Ask the Egyptian pyramid builders.

   c. No, but we hope this question gave you one last smile.

   d. Yes, 'cause any six-year-old can lead a game (fairly well) but only you can raise your leadership to an art form.

   e. *Perhaps,* if you read on (with enthusiasm).

Bonus Question: DDADA stands for:

   a. Don't Do Anything Dangerously Archaic.

   b. Describe, Demonstrate, Ask for questions, Do it, Adapt it.

   c. Dastardly Dan Ate Dirty Abalone.

   d. Delightful Dottie Ain't Doing Algebra.

   e. Make up your own.

   If you picked *e,* you showed high levels of creativity and improvement and are just the kind of leader we believe is capable of finishing this chapter and progressing to greatness (or at least to the next chapter). If you picked *b* you are probably one of those people who looks in the back of book for the answers. Realize how much you are missing in the process.

Presentation involves three main steps—recruiting, focusing, and explaining, and two sidesteps—warming up and dividing groups (if necessary).

Recruiting

Many times this won't be necessary, as you'll already have a defined group that is ready to play. But as you continue to do more events, big and small, you'll experience amorphous groups where people are (a) wandering in and out, (b) hanging out on the sidelines, (c) not sure how to join, (d) positive they don't want to play ('cause big people don't do that) and (e) many other situations. We've learned a few "tricks" that seem to work at least most of the time. It's important to remind ourselves here of the importance of invitation ("Will you come to my party?") and of creating permissions for people to take the plunge (or at least stick their toe into the water):

- Welcome them when they arrive.

- Use humor.

- Your enthusiasm and smile go a long way (remember play is a communication system). Just ask (invite them), "Hey, would you like...?"

- Hook them when they come in the door (give them something to do, put something in their hands, hand them a Frisbee and ask them if they want to catch, have them make a nametag).

- Hand them a playing card, ask them to memorize it, give it back to you and then you guess what card it was (of course you only have one card in the deck).

- Have a lot of peripheral play equipment and/or "toys and games around" that invite people to explore them on their own (e.g., face painting, scrap art, giant bubbles, stilts).

- Walk through a crowd with a rope or a parachute and say, "I really need some help. Grab on!" It's amazing how many folks will follow you.

- Run a human train (choo-choo) through the crowd and ask folks to get on board.

- Act as a "tour guide" to shy folks, walking them through the festival or event and explaining what is going on.

- Let people know that they don't have to be perfect, that the group is playing for the fun of it, that the games are easily learned, that you'd love to have them join, and that if the game isn't working for them, they can leave (it's amazing that when you give people the freedom and permission to leave they are more likely to try to join and to stay). You've created a little extra comfort zone.

- Don't use guilt trips, although John's favorite recruiting method, Chain Reaction Tag, does usually work (with a humor-filled touch of guilt). He gets a bunch of kids who want to play a game in a huddle and tells them to go to their parents (who in "proper" adult manner are standing on the sidelines) and say, "Mom, Dad, if you love me, you'll come and play with me now 'cause we really need a few more players."

- Play a game like Blob Tag (Chain Tag) where people are caught and recruited before they even know it.

So now that you've got them, what do you do? You help concentrate the play energy. This is what we call focusing or attention getting.

Focusing

In Chapter 9, *A Bigger Bag of Tricks*, we elaborate on the facilitation of Flow as one of the main goals of the play leader. Simply put, *Flow* is a high level of enjoyment, interaction and arousal, where the challenge of the activity is fine-tuned and balanced with the perceived skill level of the players. It lies in the just right place between anxiety and boredom. Dr. Mihaly Csikszentmihalyi, who has studied Flow for over 25 years, discovered one of the qualities people reported when having Flow experiences was a narrowed stimulus field and heightened level of concentration. People's focus points were not all over the map. Think about the pounding beat of an aerobics workout tape (narrowed focus) or the concentration used in a challenging video game (so much that you get "lost" in the fun).

Knowing this as a play leader is important. Using a variety of techniques and/or rituals, we can playfully *focus* people's attention and *concentrate* their collective play energy. Attention-getting techniques also help us in making our explanations and safety discussions more relaxed and less pushed. When we have people "with us" there is little need to "muscle" our leadership (yelling, using a bullhorn, or blowing an Acme Thunderer whistle in folk's ears). Focusing techniques can also be a wonderful form of microplay (the play within the play) and they save your voice so you don't talk like the Godfather at the end of the day.

Some Cheap Tricks for Attention Getting

Use Huggles (combination of huddle and hug). Bring folks close together and be in a position to be seen and heard (sit them down if you need to).

Use the Freeze and Melt technique (this is especially good with little kids). Have them practice wiggling and freezing various isolated body parts leading up to their whole self including their voice. Then have them melt and sit down. Use Merlin-like wands or gestures.

Throw a red hanky into the air and have people clap and yell when it is in the air and be silent when it hits the ground. A variation of this is when you have your arms wide open people clap loudly and when your hands are together they are silent.

Whisper (and ask people to come close enough so they can hear you).

Use a penny whistle, a kazoo, a horn, or a mouth siren. Have people know that this is a special focusing signal.

Use the Da Da Da Da Dat, Dat Dat call and response technique. Whenever you say the first part they clap and say, "Dat Dat" and are then silent. Continue this a couple of times and you've got them.

Hold up five fingers (and have the group also do this). Everyone count down loudly, "5, 4, 3, 2, 1." At "1" we're all silent.

Develop your own rituals (e.g., "When the hand goes up—the mouth goes shut, the ears are open") or a silent signal like the Girl Scout sign. Keep it light and playful.

Have little kids take a deep breath and raise both their hands over their heads. As they bring both hands down in front of them, they say, "Sssh..."

Have kids put their fingers in their ears or hands over their ears. It's amazing that when they can't hear each other they stop talking.

Let a filled balloon that you've pinched closed go off in the audience!

There are a million focusing ideas. A pioneer social recreator and professor named Alma Heaton actually wrote a whole book of them. Use your imagination and find some that work for you.

If you're one of those people who has to have a whistle and a clipboard and a megaphone and a striped shirt to prove that you're in authority, then generally you're not relying on your natural playfulness, enthusiasm, energy,

...... power to exert the authority needed to get a game going. Remember, play is a communication system. Everything you do and say gives people a message of rapport and the spirit of play *or it doesn't.* By the way, what is that ketchup spot on your sweatshirt? Gotcha!

Warmups

Every game might not need a warmup. In fact your first game or series of games might be the warmup. But we wanted to introduce this concept anyway. While you're reading this, can you do one of the following things (continue until you're finished with the warmup section):

1. Pat your head and rub your stomach or vice versa or pick two different body parts and crazy actions?

2. Sing a nursery rhyme while making a funny face?

3. Draw a picture with your nondominant hand?

4. ?

Sometimes you need *physical* warmups and stretching. Let's say you're going to play some active games and your players haven't been used to a lot of movement activity. But our concept of warmups is bigger—it is for the body *and* soul. It is to help people get into that spirit and help people connect with each other. *There is a wide range of mixers and icebreakers out there that you can choose from.* Sometimes your warmup may just be the way you sequence those first few activities. Like attention getters, this is a great opportunity for microplay. Our sense of a good warmup is that it helps people get "out of their heads" (their cognitive analytic side) and connect with their laughter, their emotions, their playful confusion, their creativity, their bodies, their integrated self (mind–body–spirit), and their intuitive right brains. And each other. A few warmups that we like to use include

- *   **The Arrows Game.** There are a lot of ways to do this. First make a chart somewhat like the one shown then point to the various arrows and have standing participants thrust their arms in the direction of the arrow and say that direction; move quickly—be tricky. Then have them thrust in one direction and say the opposite concept (e.g., thrust up, say down). Then after a few rounds of that, have them say the direction of the arrow and thrust their arms in the opposite direction. Goof with them...prior to "advanced" rounds have them raise their right hand and take a pledge that they "don't have to be perfect."

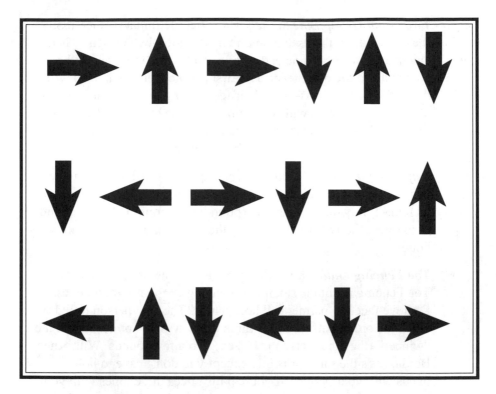

- **Touch Blue**. A quick one. "Touch blue (on someone else)...Touch red (always on someone else)...Touch a watch...Touch a shoe." After a few quick rounds ask *them* what they should touch next.

- **Cooperative Stretches and Exercises**. What ways can you and your partner figure out to warm up and stretch? Maybe I can touch your toes and you could touch mine? Maybe we can hold hands facing each other and slowly turn around together without letting go? What other ways can we think of? We might even use music.

- **Upside-Down Exercises**. Let's raise our hands to the sky, flat palms pressing upward and do 10 upside-down push-ups (regular ones, not Marine push-ups)...let me hear you count, "one, two, three." What other exercises could we turn upside down?

- **This Is My Nose**. Face your partner. Point to your elbow (or any other body part) and say, "This is my nose." The part you say (in this case, nose) your partner must point to, and in turn say a different part (e.g., "This is my butt," whereupon you'll point to your butt, and continue the interactions.

- ***Two Team Group Line Stretch***. Have people find a partner about the same size as themselves and then say good-bye to him or her. One partner will become part of one team while the other will be come part of the other team. The first people from each team will lie on the floor or grass with their feet resting on the same line; the other team members will add themselves one by one and attempt to make the longest stretched out team line while still maintaining contact with all their teammates hands or feet.

- ***Self-Doughing and Partner Doughing***. The doughing technique consists of you having closed fingers and open palms, and lightly or semi-lightly quickly tapping (pounding? chopping?) on self and/ or partner's body from the head to the toes. Kind of like working dough.

- ***Toe Fencing and/or Knee Boxing*** (Partner then Mass version). Toe Fencing is not toe stomping. Fencing is about light touches. First we face our partner and hold hands. The first person to lightly touch his or her partner's toes three times with his or her foot is the "winner" (the other person is frozen). Do a few rounds. With Knee Boxing, it's the same principle except you don't have to hold hands with your partner. If you tap his knees three times with your hand, he is frozen (of course he is trying to do this to you at the same time). After a few rounds of Partner Toe Fencing and/or Knee Boxing, why not try Mass Toe Fencing or Mass Knee Boxing? If you're touched three times by anyone, you're frozen. Watch out for high steppers and people with golf shoes!

- ***Traditional Icebreakers, Mixers, and Name Games*** (e.g., Name Bingo, Find Someone Who). Dig 'em up or make 'em up.

- ***Simple Playful Trust Builders*** (Like Touch Blue). Group builders, partner and increasingly larger group challenges.

Question: Gee Bill and John, am I getting closer to actually learning how to explain a game?
Answer: Get a partner about your size and no talking (except through your nose).

Dividing Teams

You know, the way teams have been traditionally made up (i.e., how a group gets divided into two approximately equal squads) has been one of the worst procedures known to humankind. Not playful. Not creative. Time-consuming. And often devastating to the self-image of a whole bunch of the players. Two of the most widely used traditional methods have been (a) selecting captains and having them pick the squads one by one and (b) counting off by twos. The former method is time-consuming, and generally OK, if you're one of the first ones picked. But if you're not or if you're at the tail end of the picks (say you're a slow developer or not quite as quick or coordinated or skilled as others) then it becomes a negative, self-fulfilling prophecy. You're a little hesitant, or not too sure of yourself to begin with and what do people do? They tell you (in so many ways either overtly or subtly) that they do not want you on their team because you can't chew gum and walk at the same time. It's a very cruel (and unnecessary) weeding out process. What "you" need is to be welcomed, taught, and integrated so you can progress and grow.

Counting off by twos is expressively and creatively very "flat," and it allows alert kids to "jump a space" so they'll always be with their buddies. Cliques and having your best friends on your team are OK some of the time, but it also gets in the way of experiencing the diversity of new playmates and developing your own individuality. There are alternatives to these methods and those negative experiences just don't have to happen.

There are a couple of principles that we feel are important regarding dividing teams. The first is that it should be done quickly, creatively and playfully. Again, this is an opportunity for some great microplay. So, even if you're going to "count off" why not use fruits or types of trucks or whatever (e.g., apples, peaches, pumpkin pies or dump trucks, fire trucks, milk trucks, diaper trucks). The second principle is that your method should be relatively arbitrary and random, since most accessible games don't really require equality of height, weight or athletic ability (especially if we're emphasizing playing for the fun of it). Our experience is that if you use a lot of different methods for dividing teams, and play games that don't drag on forever so people have an opportunity to be on a lot of different kinds of teams, then the issue of *us versus them* and the final score of each of those games (the "product") becomes less important and people start to focus more on the "process" of learning and enjoying. Finally, if in using any of these methods, the teams do not exactly come out even, you can always reserve the right as General Manager to make some quick shifts, if that is important (see page 36 for our cheap tricks).

OK. You've gotten their attention and you've successfully divided the teams (if necessary). You're ready to get this baby flying.

Some Cheap Tricks for Dividing Teams

Partners (the quickest best way to make two even teams). Have people get a partner about their size then say good-bye to him or her with one partner becoming a member of one team and one becoming a member of the other team (same as in Group Line Stretch warmup). Voilà! Two even teams.

Count off by Fives (the best way to break up cliques and stay a half a step ahead of 'em). Have kids line up shoulder-to-shoulder and count off by fives (apples, peaches, oranges, pumpkins, pies, and so on). You as the leader now have the option to select the ones and twos (apples and peaches) as one team or ones and threes or ones and fours or twos and threes. You have more flexibility and it's hard to out guess you! And you can use your fifth group to even out (in ability, speed, etc.) the squads if necessary.

Birthdays. The people born in the first six months of the year on one side and the second six months on the other.

Nails. Have people look at their nails. If they look at them palms up, fingers folded they are on one team; palms down, fingers straight are on the other squad.

Stand on One Foot. People standing on their left foot on one team; right foot the other.

Ducks and Cows. Have people close their eyes and whisper in their ears whether they are a duck or cow. Or they can just decide within their own minds. At a given signal, they are to keep their eyes closed and their "bumpers" up (hands in front of them) and find their fellow ducks or cows by making the noise of that animal (e.g., quack quack or moooooo) and cluster together. You can use any animals.

Mingle. Great cocktail party practice. Have the group walk around shaking hands with folks while saying "mingle mingle mingle mingle." You as the leader will say, "Groups of threes, hands on heads!" People will scurry to cluster up. Great! Let's mingle again. "Groups of five sitting down with elbows linked!" and so on until you get to the size team you want. "Groups of 20 in a shoulder-to-shoulder line!"

Presets (colors, cards, stickers, puzzle pieces). As people enter your activity, you hand each person a playing card. Later on, you can say, "All the hearts on one team." The same principle applies to hundreds of other grouping techniques. Give people different puzzle pieces. Each completed puzzle becomes a team.

Explaining

You haven't forgotten about Saying Play have you? You do remember that play is a communication system and that over 75% of human communication is nonverbal. So do you have your funny hat with you? Or a funny button or T-shirt or clown nose or a kazoo or at the very least your smiling enthusiasm and sharp sense of humor? Great, because just like everything else that has led us to this point (attention getting, team dividing) had play potential, so does *explaining.* And don't forget to model expressiveness, risk taking, foolishness, and safety...Remember, *the fun begins with you! And you can't take anyone anywhere you're not willing to go yourself!* So don't be afraid to put yourself on the line as a "demonstrator," as the first one who is "it." (*Note:* This is generally a good principle except in the case of firing squads.)

And you haven't forgotten about Teamwork and the Play Community have you (it was so long ago in *this* chapter)? So get folks involved right away in safety and in helping. In outdoor settings we like to line people up shoulder-to-shoulder and have them walk the field noting anything that they wouldn't want to step on (or in), any hazards, any chuckholes, and sprinkler heads and then cleaning up and/or marking the hazards as with a cone or Frisbee or something else that visually provides a warning. In indoor areas we like to do a similar thing but also have folks note and (re)move any hazards that may exist (e.g., papers on the floor that people could slip on or jutting tables). This involvement helps raise peoples' consciousness about safety. As a leader you never abdicate your responsibility for safety but enlisting everyone else in helping with this makes for a more caring and safe play community.

DDADA

DDADA is an acronym for all time—and most leadership settings. Yes, by now you've probably guessed that *DDADA* stands for Describe, Demonstrate, Ask for questions, Do it, and Adapt it. These procedural steps are useful whether you are leading a game, teaching arts and crafts, or conducting a business meeting. If you get in the habit of following them systematically whenever you lead a game, you'll find that your leadership and explanations will be cleaner, your games will be safer and more fun and you'll be freer to work on the adaptation and fine-tuning of the play experiences.

Describe. Have your group in formation when you're ready to begin your explanation. If it's a circle game, have them in a circle. This is essentially because games are "visual" and having them in the formation will facilitate both your explanation and the demonstration.

Be sure to have people close enough in to be seen and heard. Sit 'em down or shift the formation slightly as necessary. Does everyone have eye contact with you and vice versa? Don't forget that playful tone.

Note your position for explanation. In circle games, for example, try to be part of the circle so you have eye contact with everyone, not sucked into the middle where your back is to 50% of the players. Another crucial time to pay attention to your position is when you are outside in the sun. The sun should always be in the leader's eyes during the description. Otherwise people are so busy squinting that they might not hear your important safety rules.

Use words like "the object of the game is," "the challenge is" or "this is a tag-type game," right at the front end of your explanation to help people understand where you are going with the rest of your description.

Demonstrate. A picture is worth a thousand words, and nowhere is this more true than with games. Actually, your demonstration will be occurring simultaneously with your description so what follows in this section will actually overlap the two categories. Here are some general principles:

- Use the KISS rule (Keep It Splendidly Simple). Pick games that will allow you to do this and that the players can get into right away.

- Use your players to assist in the demonstrations. Keep your eye out for good "lightning rods" or models in the group, who will demonstrate with energy, playfulness, humor, and safety so people will get a good picture of what the action and the point is.

- Do practice rounds and slow-motion rounds if necessary, making sure everyone has the general structure before going to speed and/ or competition.

- For more complex games (e.g., Capture the Flag) break things down if you have to by using the Whole-Part Method (e.g., [a] the big picture at slow motion, [b] subparts, [c] the big picture at regular speed). With little kids sometimes you'll have to take your game back down a couple of notches for them to understand it and play it safely.

- Demonstrate safety problems and procedures and behavioral guidelines (e.g., how to properly tag versus push someone down and how to identify the potential sources of "crashes" or other danger zones in the interaction of the game). You should do this both verbally and visually to raise people's consciousness. Involve the group in identifying procedures. What would happen if...?

What should we do if...? This "buy in" makes it everybody's rules *not just yours.*

- Involve your players in deciding about rules and procedural changes in general. This is democracy in action and increases a sense of ownership in the activity.

- In your description and demonstration use stories, fantasy, analogies, themes and *rich you alls* (rituals; e.g., chanting, singing, signals) to paint a vivid, three-dimensional technicolor picture of your game. Think of yourself as the artist with a full palate of colors available to you that can convey the wonderfulness of you, the game, and the playfulness that you are initiating. Remember, play is communication. Paint a rainbow.

Ask for Questions. No matter how many times you've lead a particular game, get into the habit of asking if there are any questions. It may be clear to you; however, that confused looking guy over in the corner could botch it all up if he is not sure. Or you might have to unnecessarily stop the game when it's really rolling along at peak energy:

A good rule of thumb however is to not take too many questions. Get on with it! Too many questions could also be an indication that you need to do *another* slow-motion demonstration and/or discussion (we like to refer to that as rewind). If a player (usually this happens with kids) is asking "what if" questions ad infinitum: "what if there is a hurricane," "what if the tagger dies of a heart attack," it's time to start the game. Have the person stand next to you and say, "Stand here a bit and watch. You'll see and then you can join." Most games are visual and clarity of understanding often comes by just watching (especially if you are explaining while they are watching).

Create feedback loops and use questioning strategies so you know everyone is with you (e.g., "What is your team signal?" "How do you tag?"). Use kids' names periodically to keep 'em honest and focused (e.g., "Suzie, tell me what happens when you capture one of their players?").

Do It. Enough said.

Adapt It. So now you've got your game going (it's about time). Starting a game is not at all unlike turning on your stereo and popping in one of your favorite CDs. *Hopefully, a little more creative and playful than that* (e.g., attention getters, team divider rituals), but the metaphor is still not too bad. The "music" is supposed to serve you and the players and to provide for your enjoyment. And we know you've spent a long time thinking about your musical choice(s). The same goes for a game. Suppose it isn't working? Suppose it doesn't fit the mood? You could always pop in another CD (play a different game). But maybe all the game (music) needs is just a little adjustment of the equalizer, perhaps a little more bass, or a little less treble, maybe a little balance, and then it's just right. That is what *adaptation* is about. You'll know it when the music is right. You can tell. Or maybe you can make the game even *more* fun.

If your game needs a little fine tuning to get it into the "fun zone" for everyone, it's your job as facilitator to make that happen (of course you can, and in most cases, *should* involve your players in this). That is just what we did when we were kids. We never let the fact that we had only seven kids deter us from playing baseball (we just used fewer bases and didn't hit to right field).

There are a lot of good reasons for adaptation, including

- *Access*. That is, to let more people and more types of people (sizes, ages, abilities) join in and play.

- *Safety* (both physical and psychological). That is, to keep folks from getting hurt, or feeling left out or anxious.

- *Novelty*. You can adapt a game just to create a sense of newness.

- *Challenge*. You can modify the challenge of the activities (i.e., what it takes to potentially "succeed") whether the games be cooperative or competitive. There are a lot of other good reasons to change games but perhaps the overriding reason (which all of the above can feed) into is to adapt for greater...

- *Flow*. That is, to keep the game in the *fun zone* for the greatest number of players. Otherwise, why do it?

So if your game isn't working or if you want it to be more fun, what are some examples of some elements that you might adapt?

- Maybe you need to shrink the boundaries. Or make them bigger.

- Maybe you need more "its" (more taggers).

- Maybe you need to add more equipment (more balls, more balloons). Maybe you need less.

- Maybe you need a guessing "team" rather than just one guesser.

- Maybe you need a rule change.

- Maybe you need a new role for those who have been "eliminated" so they can still feel a part of your activity. Maybe you can find a way to eliminate elimination.

- Maybe the chasers and/or chasees need to move in a different way (e.g., hop vs. run) or the equipment has to be moved in a different way (e.g., only using feet to propel the ball or balls can be attached to wheelchairs by strings so they can be easily retrieved by the person in the chair).

- Maybe you want to change the name and fantasy of the game to suit your players or a holiday theme (e.g., Giants, Elves, Wizards or Snowmen, Santas, Reindeer instead of Rock, Paper, Scissors).

In Chapter 6, *On Games*, we'll say more about game change and creation. That is what the "newness" is all about. The possibility for endless adaptation, renewal, and re-creation.

Fine Tune as Needed

A good rule of thumb is to try each adaptation one at a time and see how it works (kids may suggest 19 changes and you'll just have to pick three). This way you'll get a clearer understanding of how a particular change altered the game. Of course, if it doesn't achieve the desired effect, you can always try something different. After a while, appropriate adaptation will become second nature and you can experiment even more. And of course if nothing works, you can always change the CD (play a different game).

Multiple Games

Up to this point, the principles that we've spoken of can apply to leading a single game or a series of games in a large or small event. In Chapter 5, *Ending It All Well*; Chapter 7, *Events or the Big Picture*; and Chapter 8, *Advanced Leadership Skills* we'll say more about "multiple games," but before closing there are a few brief thoughts about leading a series of games as opposed to a single game we'd like to suggest:

- Warmups become more important.

- Start with games that are more familiar and less strange and threatening so people feel psychologically safe (e.g., people know tag but don't know Pruie and probably might not feel that good closing their eyes and wandering around as a first game with a group of strangers). As you progress you can add ideas such as the concept that people can change and create their own games. As the play develops, you can get into whatever the group is ready for. Close your eyes and make sounds like wild Vesuvians. Who knows what that means? But by that time, they may be having so much fun they won't care.

- Use a lot of mixers, icebreakers, name games, low-key fun trust activities, and team builders early on so people have the sense of playing together and making safe contact. Generally it's important that they get the message that we're here to celebrate each other and have fun.

- Save games that have a high level of *us versus them* or perceived high competitiveness until later in the program when a sense of play community has begun to develop. There are of course exceptions to this (and every) rule. You may need to start where players *are at* (paying attention to what they are more familiar with). In some cases that might be tag games or games that have more challenge. But at least try to inject that spirit of playfulness and laughter into the experience and keep coming back to group building and bonding techniques and activities.

- Allow people to initially hide and not fear being embarrassed or singled out. If you're going to do expressive activities, have everyone do them en masse (e.g., cheers, chants, rituals) rather than starting with high individual profile games like charades.

- Start small and work up to big. Have people meet one p‹
  in partners, then threes, small groups, and lead up to big_

- Use a lot of verbal and nonverbal modeling, positive reinforcement
  (good job!) and "permissions" (to be crazy, to try, to not be perfect).

- Use some games initially as "assessment" instruments regarding
  your group (e.g., what is their level of spontaneity, humor, caution,
  willingness to touch, energy, ability to move). Plan flexibly with your
  next games based on what you observe with those initial activities.

Chapter 4

Keeping It Going
(aka, Rolling on the River)

Ride with the tide.

—Unknown

Go with the flow.

—Don't know either

Keep on keepin' on.

—Not sure

The Middle Game

Now that you have your game going well, your midgame strategy objective is to *maximize the Flow* so that you reach the highest potential for playfulness the group can obtain. The technical term for this is Big Fun!

Strange as this may seem, there are two critical, you might even say *fun*damental, concepts to be aware of during this phase of the game: s _ f _ ty and _ nth _ s _ asm. (Fill in the blanks. Answers are printed upside down at the bottom of the page [in invisible ink].) If you think these concepts seem similar to the *fun*damentals we talked about earlier, that's only because they are. Similar, true, but different.

We're going to be talking about safety in the sense of improving the "group safety," which will free each individual to go to his or her limit, which will in turn free the group as a whole to expand and deepen its levels of interaction, intercommunication, and interplay. Enthusiasm at this level focuses on group enthusiasm. The group enthusiasm or *esprit de corps* provides a context for each individual to maximize his or her own level of creativity and spontaneity. The group's enthusiasm supports and reinforces individual enthusiasm.

Safety consciousness by the group removes dangerous obstacles that impede progress, and group enthusiasm gives each player permission to go forward to newer and higher levels of playfulness. One of the ways this higher level expresses itself is that individuals and the group take on responsibility for maintaining safety and enthusiasm. The leader can encourage this behavior by reinforcing it as it occurs and by leading players toward those behaviors.

For example, someone in the group might remove a hazardous object in the playing field or ask a good question about safe playing. The leader can thank the player in front of the group and use that opportunity to ask the group if anyone else has any ideas on how to make the game safer. The leader can also ask the group if they are willing to start taking charge of safety, and then support them when they do. All these techniques help lead the players and the group to "own" the safety of all players for themselves.

The basic principle is, "Catch people doing things right and reinforce them when you do." As group members begin to look out for each other's safety and encourage each other's enthusiasm, the degree of trust and fun begins to spiral upward to a new level of group involvement. We call this level the play community.

Continue To Nurture and To Build Play Community

The *play community* is a term we first heard from Bernie De Koven to describe the entity that emerges as the group develops a sense of its own identity. Like other communities, it has a common purpose, play in this case, and a shared experience, in this case playing together. As the community develops, there begins to be an acceptance of different players as part of the group, and an acceptance of their differences as a contribution to the community. At its best, the play community becomes a celebration of how those differences help make our playing together a fuller, richer experience.

This acceptance and this honoring of differences supports a feeling of belonging, as individuals begin to identify themselves with the group. Within the community, a feeling of positive interaction evolves with shared experiences of cooperation and mutual support. There is also a growing realization that we're all working and playing together for a common goal, to have fun, and that it will be more fun if we achieve that goal together.

Though it may only last for a game or a play session, the play community often develops many of the same dynamics as the other communities in which we work and live. As the sense of community grows, the community develops its own ways to support its members. This may involve caring enforcement of the standards of the community and the rules of the game; concern for safety; and support for participation, good play, and contributions that improve the quality of play.

As the play community evolves, the role of the play leader must evolve as well. With that evolution, necessary changes take place in the relationship between the leader and the other players and between the players and the game itself. As a leader, you move from the high-visibility role of play initiator to a lower visibility role as leader–player. A level of equality develops as you step back and let the players take on leadership regarding safety and how the game will be played. As players become players–leaders, you become a leader–player. The relationship moves into balance when everyone becomes a coplaymaker at the level at which he or she is ready to participate.

The Evolving Game: The Play Community and Shared Player-Leader Roles

An interesting dynamic begins to take place as the play community develops and the leadership begins to disseminate: the relationship of the players to the game begins to change. The game, of course, is merely a vehicle for the players to reach the experience called play. Normally, games are seen as static entities with a fixed set of rules. As stated previously, we believe that the game can also be seen as a flexible structure that can be modified according to the needs of the players. As the play community takes "ownership" of the game, it often begins to change the game to make it a better vehicle for reaching the community's goals.

The game can be like buying a car. You may start with an old junker or a stripped-down model just to get around town. As time goes by, you start adding accessories—a radio, fancy hubcaps, a new paint job. At some point you may get into radical changes and drop in a new engine or turn the whole thing into a planter when it gets too old to drive. The car becomes not only a vehicle, but it becomes a statement of your creativity and unique personality.

A game can likewise be a statement of the community's creativity and personal style. The game can become not only the vehicle for reaching play, but changing the game can become a form of play by itself.

A good example of the development of a play community and the game change process occurred during a game of Frisbee Golf a few years ago. Frisbee Golf (Folf for short) is an example of game change in and of itself, combining the traditional game of golf with the relatively "new" equipment of "flying discs." We decided to modify the rules even further. There were eight of us interested in playing, so we drew on a golf variation called Best Ball and formed two teams of four. Each team would play as a unit with the best shot by any player in the unit standing as the starting point for the next throw. This made for a good deal of esprit de corps within each team and a strong but friendly rivalry between teams.

The result of this set up was a "blistering" display of Frisbee tossing during the first half of the course with the teams neck and neck at 30 and 31 shots. After a brief respite to rest our weary fingers and make color commentary on the early play, we decided to join forces on the second half of the course. It was decided that we would join forces, play "best ball" of the eight of us and we should estimate our best possible score and try to beat it. Our estimates averaged out to 26 with one radical optimist thinking we could make it in 19.

The game from that point on took on an almost magical quality. It seemed that on every series of throws a different player stepped up and pulled out a magnificent shot. Even if the first seven throws were mediocre or worse, we were all sure that the eighth player would somehow lift the team with a shot made from heaven. And it would happen.

The upshot of the game was that we returned to our starting point not just bettering our estimate, we more than cut it in half! Our total score for the second half of the course was 12! We far exceeded the greatest expectation that any of us had.

So what does this tell us. It might be a testimonial to the fact that by playing together we can do far better than playing against each other. It showed us that when we all started to play together as a community, we all started to support each other, root for each other and try to help each other in whatever way we could, which seemed to help each of us perform better. It also showed us that when we were in the game for the fun of playing together, we felt we had the right to change the game to make it work better for us. In changing the game we gave ourselves the opportunity to create an experience that was really challenging, outrageously fun and truly a Flow experience. I think if you asked anyone who played in that game that day that he or she would recount it as one of the most significant play experiences in his or her life.

This Frisbee Golf game is a good example of how the interaction of the play community and the game can take the play experience to an almost transcendent level that brings the players even closer together. The best way we know of to attain that high level of playfulness is to support the development of the play community. The key to developing the play community is the willingness of the play leader to empower the players by shifting to a lower visibility role.

Play Exercise: The Roles and Qualities of the Leader

Draw a line down the center of a sheet of paper. In the next three minutes write as many roles as you can that you think the play leader might take (e.g., butcher, baker, candlestick maker—just kidding): teacher, comedian, coach, etc., on the left side of your paper. Go for 20 good ones. Now that you have 25 (we are watching and looking for extra effort), on the right-hand side list as many qualities of a play leader that will be important for success (e.g., sense of humor, flexibility, being organized, assertive). Get at least 26. Look at both lists. When and why might these roles and qualities be important?

High Viz Versus Low Viz

One way to categorize roles a play leader might take is to distinguish between ones that are *high visibility* and ones that are *low visibility.* In the beginning of a game, you as a leader probably need to be very high viz. At that point people need to recognize you as a leader to focus the attention of the group, gather them together, explain the rules, and review the safety considerations.

As you move into the midgame and the activity of the game kicks in, you as a leader need to drop back and lead by example. During this phase you can model "well-playedness," another Bernie De Kovenism. Your demonstration of good play, safe play, and support of others will encourage the rest of the players to do the same. You can also step out of the way to allow others to take a leadership role.

Initially, as questions come up about the game, the group will probably turn to you and ask for an answer, "What do we do if this happens?" As a low-viz leader, you can turn the question around, use the "boomerang" technique, and say, "That's a good question. What do all of you think should happen?" Let the group start to make the decisions. As a leader you take the role of *process manager* helping them navigate the process of decision making, but letting them make the final decisions.

It's easy once you get good at being a high-viz leader—humorous, knowledgeable and organized—to become trapped in the role of the "star." People like stars. It's easy for a group to let someone else (like you) run the show, particularly if it's a good show. However, it very quickly moves from being a game to which everyone contributes into entertainment for the players-audience and an ego trip for the entertainer–leader. It's a real challenge for you as a leader to let go of the ego boost for yourself and start boosting other people's egos. When you do that, you start to realize that there is a much greater level of satisfaction that comes from seeing other people blossom and develop. You also find out that the game can be a lot more fun for you when there are other equals helping to create it.

Sometimes the transition from a leader-directed game to a community-directed game can be a little rocky. There will often be a temptation to jump back in and take charge to insure that the game "works." Sometimes that will be the right thing to do and sometimes it will be important to let the group work through the rough times as best they can, even let the game break down, so that the group will start to take charge. Remember to take it easy on yourself as well. Handing the leadership of the game off well is another facilitation skill, just like gathering people together, presentation or safety monitoring. The more you practice transferring leadership, the better you'll get at it, and the more fun it will become for you.

Safety

One area where you always need to be able to jump back from the low-viz role is safety. Even if the group seems to be doing well in taking charge of the game, you have bottom-line responsibility for the safety of the group and its members. If a situation arises that can't be handled in a less obvious way, you need to step in before someone gets hurt. You can give away responsibility for the players having fun but you can't give away responsibility for the players being safe. A guideline here might be that if you have to step back into a high-viz role try and do it in a way that continues to empower the group, and try and make the intervention in a way that you can get in and out of the high-viz role as quickly as is possible and still meet the safety demands of the situation (check out our cheap tricks).

When working with safety situations, it's very important to be conscious of the way you present an issue or the way you talk about it. That includes your tone of voice, your stance, your relationship to the group, your use (or lack thereof) of humor. Although humor can be used in talking about safety or making people aware of safety, it has to be used so that it adds to rather than subtracts from the message. People must still be clear that safety is important and not to be trivialized. Other times, you may want to change the tone of voice into your "serious" tone so that people know by your tone, by the pace of your talking, by the words you choose, or by the way you look at people in the group that this is serious, this is something that everybody needs to be concerned about.

An example of using your voice for safety comes from a situation where you look across the field and see an inexperienced leader working with a group of teenagers. One teen has gone from crawling on the giant six-foot Earthball to trying to stand on it. As you begin a cheetah-like sprint across the open field, you yell, "Hold It!" with your best kiai elephant bellow—a voice trained to stop the charge of a raging lion, immobilizing him instantaneously. All eyes in the group of Earthball players immediately stop and focus in your direction as the youth atop the ball descends to the ground.

Arriving at the Earthball, you assume your calm, fire-captain-speaking-to-young-recruits voice. In a comradely, but definitely commanding tone, you explain, "Yeah, I know it looks like it might be really fun to have someone try and stand on the ball. And it definitely would be a challenge to do that.

Five Cheap Tricks (More or Less) for Managing Safety

2. ***Freeze and Think***. This works especially well with younger kids, but it can be used with people of all ages. When you see a safety problem that needs immediate attention, yell, "Freeze!" at the top of your lungs. From childhood games of Freeze Tag and lots of cops and robbers movies, we're all conditioned to stop dead when we hear that word. Within seconds you'll have a group of frozen statues. Now that you're very high viz, you can ask the group if anyone noticed any particular safety hazards that need to be remedied. Be sure to thaw people out so they can discuss ways to solve the safety problem.

   Once you get the players to identify safety problems and ways to deal with them, they start to take ownership of the solutions. Usually, if they generate the solution, they will be much more responsible about maintaining it than if you just tell them what to do. It's another form of empowerment.

1. ***Freeze***. The short form of Freeze and Think, this works well when the action is getting a little too wild and you need a slow down or there is some pattern going on that needs to get broken up. It's often effective with 8- to 12-year-old boys, and/or high-energy short-attention span types.

   For younger kids who are really amped up, you can practice freezing and thawing one body part at a time. By the time you work your way through the whole body they will think that was the whole game.

3. ***Stop, Look, Listen, Feel***. A slightly more subtle version of Freeze and Think. Have the players stop, look around and talk about what they see. Then have them close their eyes and talk about what they hear. This will usually start to calm things down dramatically. You can end with asking people to talk about how they are feeling or ask leading questions such as, "Anybody feel like the game was getting out of control?" And, you can end by asking people to think about how to make the game safer.

   A great way to use this technique is to introduce it early on as a sensory awareness game and then to recycle it periodically through the play session to build group awareness. It becomes a built-in tool for safety when and if you should need it for that. When people are stopped with their eyes closed, you can use questioning strategies to ask them to visualize what might happen if a certain safety problem went unchecked. You can also ask them to visualize potential solutions to the problem.

Five Cheap Tricks (More or Less) for Managing Safety (continued)

4. ***Anticipation***. When you perceive the potential for a safety problem in the middle of a game, it's a good time to use "what if" questions to help the group anticipate problems and solutions before they are needed. Just anticipation may allow you to avoid the problem altogether. In other words, be a good risk manager.

    You can also use anticipatory questions with your problem child types by asking them, "What do you think could happen if...?" On a good day they may come up with some positive answers. On a not so good day they will probably come up with some brilliant response such as, "I don't know," at which point you can ask the rest of the group to help out with suggestions. The trick here is to "give notice" that you realize where the problem is stemming from and yet not put the player(s) so much on the spot that it be comes punitive.

4.5 ***The Ripple Stop Technique***. This is a great one for high-energy activities and was mentioned briefly in Chapter 2, *The Fundamentals of Play Leadership*, but now that we're going full tilt boogie, it's important to reiterate. After you've gone through identifying safety hazards with the players, explain that to keep things safe, whenever anyone notices a safety problem or feels that anyone's body is in jeopardy he or she is to yell "Stop!" Whenever anyone hears the word *stop* he or she is to stop whatever he or she is doing and yell "Stop," also until everyone is yelling stop and no one is moving. In this way, a very large group can be brought to a screeching halt in a few seconds.

    It's important to cheerlead the group through several practice rounds before resuming play and perhaps one during play just to keep people alert. It's also important that everyone agree not to use the Ripple Stop Technique for strategic purposes but only for legitimate safety ones. It's important to keep everyone aware and following the safety "stop" rule. The Ripple Stop Technique is particularly valuable in "soft war" games like wrestling or aggressive tag-type games, where there is a lot of physical contact and challenge and aggression being played out. People need to know that, as they are doing this, they have some safety check to control the action and stop it if they feel the need to. It becomes like ripples in a pond: 1 person starts it; then 3 people hear that person yelling it and start to yell it also; then 10 people; then 30 people. Pretty soon, what ever the group size, the group has stopped, and the safety issue is addressed.

Five Cheap Tricks (More or Less) for Managing Safety (continued)

5. ***Exaggeration***. This is a little bit like anticipation. You see something that might become or is already a small problem. Take a time-out with the group and exaggerate what potentially could happen, but in a realistic way. Say, "What if this, this, this, this occurred? We could have this terrible tragedy." Say it in such a way that the group can understand that you're playing with it and that you also take it seriously— that nobody would want this terrible tragedy to happen, so maybe nobody wants the smaller problem to happen, either.
   A good way to do this sometimes is...

6. ***Slo-Mo Modeling***. Acting out or asking members of the group to act out a potential safety hazard (e.g., in a running game, collisions between two people running in different directions) in slow motion helps to focus the group members' awareness. Have them act it out in stop-action slow motion, like they are in a movie. Over 12 or 13 seconds, they collide, start falling to the ground and spend another 3, 4, 5, 6, 7 minutes dying dramatically. Meanwhile, the whole group gets the message, "Yeah, we don't really want that to happen." At the same time, it slows down the pace for the whole group.
   After doing a Slo-Mo Model of the safety hazard, you might want to ask somebody else in the group to do a Slo-Mo Model of how the interaction might have occurred safely, in a different way.

7. ***Lecture***. When all else fails, use the old safety lecture—not to blame people, berate them or dress them down, but just to talk about the importance of safety and how it affects the group and individuals within the group. Hit on the higher values and how being safe can contribute to play, as well as how not being safe can deprive us of the opportunity to play. Try to tap into people's higher aspirations, rather than into their fears. But if you really need to, tap into their fears.

8. ***Last But Not Least: Pledges***. The pledge is a really cute way to get people focused on a safety aspect. Ask them to raise their left hand and repeat after you: "I pledge to do my best to do my duty to the State of Maine and the government of the Island of Aruba, to make sure that I personally will play this game safely. I will not run into other people. I will not throw things at them above the shoulders or below the waist. I will not _____ and I will be careful, think about other people, take care of myself and my fellow players, have a good time and be totally safety conscious all the time. Thank you and good night."

Five Cheap Tricks (More or Less) for Managing Safety (continued)

By doing this in a humorous but clear way, it gets people to recognize what the safety issues are and take responsibility for them. Even though it's actually a lecture, it's participatory. They have a sense that, "Well, since I pledged to do it, I guess I ought to do it." If nothing else, you get to stop the game if a problem occurs and say, "Excuuuse me! Did we pledge to play safely? Yeess. Are we playing safely? Nnnoo. Do we need to do something differently? Yeess." And so on.

9. ***The Double Check*** (just when you thought it was safe to stop reading the cheap safety tricks). The Double Check is a way of polling the group to confirm everyone is aware of the safety issues. After you've had a lecture or discussion about safety issues, you can ask people two questions. The first question: "Is everybody aware now of the safety issues and willing to be careful as we play with each other?" Generally, everyone will nod their heads; some people will be off in space. That's when you hit 'em with the Double Check and ask them: "Is there anybody in this group who is not aware of the safety issues and/or not willing to play safely and be careful with everybody else in the group?" Long pause; everybody looks around, looks at each other to see if there's anybody who's not willing to do that. Generally, nobody would say that in front of the rest of the group, except one person may playfully say, "Well, I'm not..." At that point, everyone has given their commitment to play safely and you can move on.

10. ***The Small Example***. I know we said the Double Check was the very, very last, but forget it, there's more: At any time, when you see a Small Example, take advantage of that. Ask the people involved if they mind being a safety example for the group. Use the example by saying, "Now in this case, fortunately, the people involved were in enough control that they didn't get hurt or this didn't turn into a situation where somebody got hurt. But it might have." Then ask them if they have any suggestions on how other people could avoid getting into that problem situation.

11. ***Safety Task***. Safety task is setting up an agreed upon cue so that if something happens or if there's something going on at any point in time, the leader or anybody in the group acting as a leader can call for a safety task to occur. For example, it might be "Blue Line." When anybody yells, "Blue Line!" everybody in the group has to get to the blue line or the designated spot right away. It's a great way for people to break up the pattern if they see that something unsafe is going on. (Did you notice that there were more than five?)

And the possibility for someone to be seriously injured is extremely great. Earthballs are not known for their balance and the ground that we're playing on is not known for its evenness. So, even if a person was particularly astute and agile, as I'm sure this young man is, the chances are that the Earthball could take a bad bounce, that someone could slip, injure numerous bones in his body, and it is too high a risk for any of us to want to take. Thanks for your support—I appreciate you all being willing to play safely and take care of each other. We want to keep you in top shape to be able to play longer, play harder, and have more fun in the long run. Thanks again; feel free to crawl around on the ball, roll on it, as long as you're spotting each other and making sure that everybody is taking charge of everybody else's safety. That works out just fine. Thanks again."

As you step aside with the inexperienced leader and assume the voice of the mentor-with-paternal-warmth, say, "Now, you have great enthusiasm and you're really able to bring people together and energize them to play hard." Then shift to your steely-coldness-of-the-senior-surgeon-focusing-on-a-neurosurgical-mistake-by-a-young-trainee voice, convey the coldness of a samurai blade about to descend and slice one's head in two. Gaze directly into the soul of this leader and say, "You can never, ever let anyone try to stand on an Earthball. You're the only person in the game that's going to stand between the player's excited desire to do something tremendously fun and absolutely dangerous and the player actually *doing* that dangerous thing. He might hurt himself, perhaps in a way that could damage him for the rest of his life. You *always* and *everywhere* have to be the bottom line on safety, even when you think it can be done safely, you have to be in a position to say 'No, it's not worth the risk.'"

Shifting to a warmer but still definite tone, you conclude with a statement like, "You're a good leader and you're going to get better. And, if you're lucky and can learn from this without anyone having gotten hurt, then you'll have gained a really great opportunity and a good lesson. So, see if you're able to take this and translate it into safety for the rest of this activity and the rest of your life. Good luck—go for it." And you walk away. This is not a point at which there's any opportunity for discussion.

Your voice and the way you use it is probably one of the most powerful and versatile techniques that you as a leader are going to have in your bag of tricks. Altering the tone and style of voice that you use will give messages on a nonverbal level, as well as a verbal level. Those messages will convey a lot about the role and the authority with which you are speaking at that moment. Just as an actor has to learn to use the voice to create characters that are real and compelling to an audience, you have to learn to use voice in a way that is effective in shaping the experience of the players to create the maximum possibility for play.

As Ultimate Safety Monitor, there are two questions you can ask your-self: If not me, then who? And if not now, then when? If not me, then who? asks, If I'm not going to address this safety issue at this point, who is going to? If there's someone else that will address it or that you can encourage to address it, then it's great to empower that person and thereby model for the rest of the group that all the players are responsible. If you don't think any-one else is going to address it or that you can get to address it, then you have to address it. If you determine that it's an issue that can't be addressed in the future, and that it's a compelling safety issue that could put someone at risk, then the time to address the issue is *right now*—as soon as you are aware of it—in the best way you can.

You can also establish some personal criteria for intervening in situations for safety. One is the frequency with which some activity is going to cause an injury, even if it's a slight injury. Perhaps you want to play a running game, but the only area you have to play on is very uneven and you find that it's common that people start to twist ankles or step in holes. Even though the injuries are not that great, they seem to be happening pretty frequently, then it's probably a good indication that you have to come up with a different way to play the game or a different game for the setting.

The opposite end of the spectrum is that you may have an activity where it's generally very safe to play but the downside risk is that someone could get hurt very severely. An example of this was a game that someone once suggested that involved throwing a gym mat into the swimming pool. The mat created a floating island in the pool that players could actually climb onto and crawl around on. Eventually, the activity became an aquatic version of King of the Mountain, which was a lot of fun. However, as the game got more exciting and people got rougher and more focused on the game, the risk arose that someone could become trapped under the mat, swallow water, panic, and that the other members of the group would be too excited to no-tice. Potentially, someone could drown and no one would notice. Now, the chance of this happening was pretty remote. However, the severity of the possible accident, where someone could actually lose his or her life or have a near-death experience, was such that it really wasn't worth playing the game.

It's important to recognize that there are always risks and you can't play together without risks of some kind of injury, whether it's physical or emo-tional. We have to work on doing our best to minimize the risks and take care of situations as early as possible so that, hopefully, nobody gets hurt and, if somebody does get hurt, he or she isn't hurt seriously. Most of the informa-tion that we've been talking about in regard to safety in this chapter has been oriented around physical safety. However, *the principles apply equally to the idea of psychological or emotional safety.* As a leader, whether you're in a high- or low-visibility role, it's important to recognize that you have an obligation to support the psychological safety of every player in the game.

A very general way in which we can do that is to become a Process Guardian for the group process. That means that we can be responsible for maintaining a good, fair, and impartial process in the play community. We can help players to become conscious through strategically asked questions of the process or the way in which they are playing together. Particularly, we can help them to recognize key points to help them play well together or factors that might lead to a breakdown of the group's playfulness. Remember the Process Guardian's Code: "Protect the innocent, encourage the weak, restrain the manipulators. Have a good time."

We also want to empower the other players in the game to become Process Guardians as well. It may take a little while for them to start to recognize this process in their behavior. They oftentimes will ask questions or make comments that indicate, although they may not be calling it *process,* they are aware of what's going on in the dynamics of the game.

In many ways, during this middle part of the game, your job is to be like a whitewater kayaker. If you're riding a river, imagine that you're going through lots of whitewater and the river's strong enough that you can actually ride your kayak through. As you do that, you're constantly shifting your balance, constantly taking different roles, moving back and forth, from side to side, balancing. Change versus stability. Balancing enthusiasm and safety. Balancing high and low visibility. Empowerment versus control.

All of these things are elements that you have to practice in navigating the whitewater. Sometimes you get flipped over. That's inevitable; you have to be willing to right yourself, going for it again and again. As you do, you learn to read the water before you get to it. You begin to be able to shift your balance and paddle strokes in more subtle ways and you get dumped a lot less often. Here are some guidelines to keep in mind as you work on your role as Process Guardian:

Keep the Agreements on the Rules...or, Consciously and Clearly Choose to Change the Rules. This is a good point to talk about the concept of cheating versus creative play. Sometimes it begins to look like someone is cheating within the game, but it's actually a good idea for a new way to play the game. The person is just expressing the fact that he or she has come up with some new, creative way to get around a rule actually making the game more fun. If that's happening, then it's great to validate it; maybe the group wants to decide it's OK to use the innovation. It's important, though, to be clear that it's what the group wants to do because, if the group doesn't want to do that and that person's behavior or strategy is taking advantage of other players in the game, then other people will perceive it as "cheating." That will soon create problems within the group that will lead to No Fun.

Check for Clarity. As we mentioned, periodically, different things—whether it is maneuvers people make or strategies they start to take on—may start to add confusion about how the game is being played. It's important to check in and determine whether everyone is clear on the rules, the objectives and the agreements about how things are being done. This helps create security for those people who are less assertive about stepping out for themselves and saying, "I don't understand what's going on here."

Invite Participation. As Process Guardian, you can ask, "Is there anyone else who wants to add anything to the discussion?" Or you can be even more direct. Find the person who's quiet or shy and say, "Arnold, do you have any ideas or anything you want to say about what's going on before we continue playing?" Try to make it as easy as possible for those people to get a chance to participate. Make sure everyone is heard, that everyone has a chance for input. Gradually, by doing that, those people will start to feel safe enough to come out more and participate more. Also, other people in the group—even the ones who tend to be outgoing and assertive—will realize there are people out there taking care of them. Maybe they'll start to learn—and you can encourage them to learn—those types of behaviors themselves. Let them become outgoing about being Process Guardians rather than just focusing on their own needs all the time.

Check for the Bellwethers, Lightning Rods, and Superstars. In each group, there are what we call *bellwethers* that signal changes in the weather that may come about soon. In this case, it may be the highly energetic kid who gets bored easily. In observing bellwethers, you can tell whether the game is slowing down and losing its juice and whether it might be time to come up with some kind of change. On the other hand, it may be the person in the group that tends to be very cautious and starts to drop out whenever the game starts to get a little bit out of control. That person also can be a good indication that the game may need a little more stability. There are a couple of ways to deal with the bellwethers. First, check to have a sense of whether there is anything imminent that needs to be done to create safety or stability in the game. Second, look at the possibility of some individual coaching to help players cope within the play experience. Walk up to them individually in a low-visibility manner so it doesn't disrupt the rest of the players and see if there is anything they can use in support from you that will help them participate more fully in the game. Your highly energetic "go for it" lightning rods and superstars may also signal you that it's time to change the game, if their play is becoming obviously flat.

Be Careful of Boredom. We've talked about a lot of the kinds of safety factors that may come from things getting too wild and out of control. There are also safety factors that come when the game starts to get boring. Sometimes a game can go on even when the interest level starts to go down because people are running on the extra energy they had when the game was exciting and there was a lot of juice to it. However, when people are bored, they can make different kinds of mistakes. Sometimes, it's a physical mistake based on inattention that causes someone to get hurt; sometimes it may be an emotional mistake that involves one person saying something to someone else that hurts that person's feelings or someone acting in a way that causes him or her to get ostracized by other people in the group. These behaviors come out of an irritability or a carelessness that comes from the fact that people are getting bored. So the Process Guardian can start to notice when boredom is creeping in and see if there is a way to encourage behavior that will create more excitement, boosting the enthusiasm and energy level back up.

We've been talking for a long time about safety factors with an emphasis on how, even as you make an overall shift to a lower visibility leadership role, you may have to take a high-visibility role in regard to safety. What we want to reemphasize is that the ideal is for the play community and for the team to own the responsibility for its own safety. As you develop mastery as a leader, you develop the ability to encourage others and lead others to take on the safety role from your low-visibility position. As a less experienced leader, you have to take this role on yourself from a more high-visibility position. The best leader, the Chinese sage once said, is the one that people barely know exists. If people take responsibility and own their own safety, they begin to own their own empowerment. As they do that, they will gain greater satisfaction. As they gain greater satisfaction, they will experience more Flow and Bigger Fun which is, after all, What It's All About!

Support Great Playing

We all know what a great play is when we see it in a sport with which we are familiar. In basketball we've seen Michael Jordan steal the ball, break toward the basket at his end of the court, drive between four other players, go up for the shot being nearly blocked by a taller man, double-pump fake, bring it back under his arm, toss it behind his back off the glass of the backboard and drop it through the hoop as he comes down on the other side of the court (somehow). The crowd stands and cheers, whistles, yells wildly, and screams.

In golf, you might have a somewhat different display. A player lines up for a particularly difficult sand trap shot. The crowd is gathered around the green in hushed anticipation. It seems the entire crowd is holding its breath. The player focuses, concentrates, drops his shoulder, leans into the swing, the ball goes up, it is in the air, a beautiful arc, it comes down, bounces once, twice, rolls toward the hole and—incredibly—curves three inches to the left and drops into the hole for an eagle on a par four hole! The crowd erupts into quiet applause, each person placing three fingers softly against the palm of the opposite hand—the traditional roar of approval in golf.

In some games, like tennis, for years it wasn't even considered appropriate to applaud when someone made a good shot or a daring save. One can imagine Wimbledon 30 years ago, someone making a spectacular diving save to get a ball, dropping it back over the net for a winning shot. The player on the other side of the net looks over in polite formality saying, "Well-played, old chap. Nicely done."

As mentioned before, Bernie De Koven authored a book called *The Well-Played Game*. In it, Bernie talks about the quality of *well-playedness* in many different aspects of games. It is an aspect of playing that is important to recognize and realize that well-playedness can be found in any type of game, whether it is a singing game, a rhyming game, a field game, or a board game. In any way in which we play together, there are great plays that people can make. Those great plays are the ones that ultimately contribute to everyone having a better time.

As a leader, we can create Big Fun in the game by promoting well-playedness. The first step toward this is recognizing it when we see it. Then, once we've recognized it, using that moment of recognition to acknowledge the well-playedness of it to the player or players in the game. As we do this, we start to educate and teach all the players about what are well-played games and teach them to support each other and recognize and acknowledge each other for playing well. Again, as people start to learn to take care of each other and to support each other for playing well, it becomes a mutual admiration society. The good feelings start to spiral upward, creating more of a sense of fun and enthusiasm within the play group. For people, public recognition of making a good play adds to their sense of self-esteem, their sense of being wanted, invited, cared about, welcomed, and empowered. Naturally, this leads to lots more satisfaction and a greater experience of the Flow.

Bending, Shaping, Changing, and Playing Well

New, creative ideas and ways to play the game often lead to new levels of possibilities for Flow maintenance or higher levels of fun rather than the players going into a state of boredom. Sometimes, breaking a rule benefits the whole community by showing a new way of playing the game nobody thought of before. At one time all the plays were running plays in football. Then, someone got the bright idea that you could throw the ball forward and it would make for more excitement. Today, some of the greatest excitement in the game comes from the long bombs. At one time there was no three-point basket. When someone came up with that idea, if everyone said, "Oohh, that's not real basketball; that's no way to do it," and the change were not made, we wouldn't have the excitement of a team that's down by two points with three seconds left to play and someone launches a long shot from beyond the three-point line and manages to pull out victory for his or her team with a spectacular shot.

Another example of creative rule changing adding to the Flow of a game is an actual situation where, as a way to gather the group together, the group members were asked to step across a tile floor of 12-inch squares making sure that, as they moved, no one stepped on any of the cracks between the tiles and kept their feet well within the squares. Of course, as people started to move closer together, someone began to use the old children's rhyme of "Step on a crack, break your mother's back; step on a line, break your mother's spine." As the group members began milling around each other, the game became how can we move around in a group without stepping on a line. All of a sudden one player, who happened to be a very agile basketball player, came by a fairly big guy who happened to be a football player. She suddenly faked toward him just when he wasn't expecting it; he stepped onto a crack. Of course, he thought this was tremendously unfair but, after a moment, he realized this was an opportunity for a new level of play. He called for a round of Snap-Clap (applause) and the basketball player who had innovated this new rule proposed that the group try a new game which was, without touching anyone, to see if, as you moved around, you could fake people into making a misstep and stepping onto a crack. It became a quiet but energetic game of Dodge and Fake that was competitive but playful at the same time.

As a leader, it's important to be open to the change in the moment and not say, "Well, wait a second; this is the way we're playing the game. Let's stick to that." Instead, in this instance, realize that the group can be energized by shifting into a more competitive phase of the game. At the same time, it was important to recognize the basketball player for her innovation which might have been called *cheating* in the first level of the game, but really became the norm of well-playedness in the second level of the game. By recognizing her, it set a pattern that said to everybody else in the game, it's good to come up with ideas for how to do things differently—everybody pays attention to you and thinks you are terrific.

Encouraging creativity and variations not only gets people involved on a physical level, but also gets them involved on a mental, creative level as well. It starts to hook them into the spontaneity of their spirit as they make a shift from being participants in the game, consumers of a game, to being producers of the game. As we know, it's generally more exciting when you are doing something in which you have a personal investment, rather than doing something that somebody else has provided for you and all you have to do is go through the motions.

Game Change Quality and Process

We've emphasized that one of the key ways to keep the level of play quality up in a game is by changing the game. We change games for lots of different reasons. Sometimes it's to promote greater safety or more participation, to add challenge, to simplify the game, to add excitement or, sometimes, just for the newness of the game. Ultimately, the reason we're changing the game is for the fun of it—to add more fun and quality to the players' experience. Which is different than changing your socks or underwear (usually done for the health of it). When we're changing games, it's good to remember to change just one element of the game at a time to create some stability so people don't lose track of what is going on and start getting anxious. It might be changing one rule or some other element of the game, like the fantasy. For example, we might play Rock, Paper, Scissors and then decide, well, we've done this for a while—let's try something different and change to a game of Tiger, Man, Camera, which is really the same game with different symbols. Or we might get into sort of a role play; that's how a game called Giants, Elves, Wizards was created. People acted out different characters; one character still had the power to beat another which was balanced by being able to be conquered by the third character. Or we might take a game like Crows and Cranes, which is a team tag game where the Crows try to tag the Cranes or vice versa before they make it back to a safety zone. If it's Valentine's Day, maybe we'll change the theme of the game and the two team names to Hugs and Kisses. All of a sudden, the game has a newness and excitement to it because of the topicality of the game. People come up to you and make remarks like, "You know, I played a game similar to this one time, but I think it was a little different. It seemed to involve birds or something." Or an old timer will come up to you with a twinkle in her eye and say, "This isn't a new game; I played it when I was a kid, only we called it Crows and Cranes. But I like this Hugs and Kisses version better."

Sometimes, changing the game becomes the game itself. One time, we were in a workshop and we brought everybody together in a huddle inside the circle at the center of the basketball court. We said, "Are you ready for a new game?" Everybody said, "Yeah!" So we said, "OK; here's a totally new and different game." And we introduced a game that they hadn't played yet called Everybody Is It Tag, where everybody was "it" and, when you were tagged, you became frozen. The idea was to be the last person unfrozen. So, we played around within the inner circle; it was a pretty small space and a whole round took only three or four seconds. We figured that was just a practice to give people the idea.

In introducing round two, we said, "So, are you ready for a completely new and different game?" Everybody said, "Yeah! Sure! Why not?" So, we introduced Everybody Is It Tag again with exactly the same rules, except we widened the boundary out by about 10 feet. When people realized that it was really the same game and we'd only changed the boundaries, but were calling it a totally new and different game, they all laughed but went ahead and played it anyway and had a good time.

This began a trend. So, we said, "How about a totally new and different game?" Everybody said, "Yeah!" Then we would change just one more rule. Maybe allowing people to be tagged twice or to have wounds and cover the wounds with their hands until they didn't have any more hands left to cover the wounds, then they'd be frozen. Or we gave people partners. Or say that they were only frozen for a limited amount of time. Eventually, we came up with about 15 different variations. Every time we introduced a variation (or someone came up with a variation), they'd say, "I've got an idea for a totally new and different game." By the time we finished with Everybody Is It Tag, Version 23(b)(12), the real exciting part of it was somebody coming up with a new and different way to do the same thing. That became the game.

Changing Channels: A Totally Different Game (Really)

Everybody Is It Tag shows a good transition between playing one game and playing serious multiple games. Oftentimes, in a play session, we have time for more than one game. It's not just a matter of changing that game and coming up with variations on it. It's also a matter of changing from one game to a completely different game. Earlier, we talked about the play leader as an artist who has a range of different colors that can be added to a game through the use of fantasy or ritual, or different ways of using the rules to add different qualities and flavors to a game. You can also see a series of games as one big game with a Flow of its own. Each of the games you introduce into that sequence of games has a color of its own, a flavor and style of its own. You, as the artist, are going to be mixing and matching those colors, flavors, and styles to create an overall artistic, playful effect.

In mixing, matching, and sequencing different games, you want to look at not only how the individual games are played, but how they relate to each other. What are the transitions from game to game? Do those occur smoothly and evenly or are they kind of jagged and abrupt? As a Flow engineer, you want to look at how you can maintain a high-level Flow as you change from one game to another. You don't want to start a new game, build the excitement level, keep it up during the middle of the game as it starts to wane, stop the game, go dead in the water, and then have to start the Flow up again. Instead, the Flow is maintained at a nice even, high level with occasional ups and downs, never bottoming out as you move from game to game.

We'll say more about the practical implications of Flow Theory in Chapter 8, *Advanced Leadership Skills*, but for now, in organizing your series of games, there are a few principles to keep in mind:

- *Variety*. Do some games that give people a range of different things to do so they don't get too much into a rut. They want to experience different kinds of flavors: some might be fast paced, some might be slower paced, some might be quiet games, and some might be active games.

- *Balance*. Look for games that help balance each other so that, after you've done a couple of active games and people are starting to become physically tired, you balance that with a mental game that gets people intellectually excited and allows them to rest their bodies. Balance other aspects of the game: some competitive games and some cooperative games; circle games with line games; and outside games with indoor games.

- *Continuity*. There sometimes is a value to having a central theme that coordinates all the games. It might be related to a holiday like Halloween, with a whole range of monster-type games—Vampire, Chiller, Blob Tag, Hide 'n' Go Seek in the Dark. A theme can help create a sense of continuity as you segue from one activity to the next.

- *Build Up and Break Down*. It is good in a sequence of games to start with some of the simpler, more basic activities first (maybe even in pairs of small groups) and then build up to the more complex ones (maybe in large groups). As people start to get worn out, finish with some fun but simple exercises that aren't too difficult for people to get into and that represent nice closure activities so that people go away relaxed and able to focus on the connection between themselves and the other people, rather than on the complexity of the game. It also may mean that the level of complexity can take place on an emotional level, as well as on a rule level. We usually start with warm-up games, icebreakers that help people get to know each other and relax being around each other, then we move into the more challenging games that involve trust or communication or physical contact or intimacy. Then end with games that are simple but bring people together with a sense of awareness of the whole and a simple recognition of each other. This is a nice way to say good-bye to folks at the end of a play session. So remember, start with the least threatening, least difficult activities and move into the more challenging and end with the simple but profound.

Look for opportunities for play in the spaces between the games. Just because the game stops doesn't mean the play has to stop. You might be sitting in a circle on the ground in a quiet game and you are ready for an active game. Instead of having everybody just stand up and walk over to the playing field, you can say, "OK! Let's have the group stand up! How about if everybody grabs the hands of the person next to them and, without putting any hands on the ground, pull each other up to a standing position." Well of course half the time, it doesn't work and people fall over each other—that becomes the play. Or some folks get up easily and you encourage them to help the laughing, struggling others—you've just reinforced caring, helping behaviors.

So think about what creativity might take place in the sequence. A circle becomes a line; a line very easily becomes a train; a train choo-choos along the track; the train brakes with a loud hiss as it comes into the station; at the station people meet and greet their friends, families, and lovers; the train pulls out of the station. The train becomes a blind walk; the blind walk becomes a game of Stop, Look, and Listen. So, all of a sudden, we've gone from a circle to a line to a train to a game without ever turning it into a well-defined, structured activity, but at the same time creating lots of wonderful moments for creativity and play.

Another thing you can do is use an individual's movement from one place to another for a change in games to initiate play. To get from the sidewalk to the baseball diamond, you may have to cross the Poison Peanut Butter Pit. You may have to create rules for the group on how to do that. Or just have them imagine people running across hot coals to get there. All of these things can create playful moments and create ways for the group to interact and come up with ideas on how to solve problems. Problem solving becomes a game in and of itself.

In using the spaces between games, think about maximizing the activity of the players. Instead of finishing a parachute game and saying, "OK, let's play another game," and having everybody stand around while you stuff the parachute in the bag and walk the group over to a new area—not much is happening while you're walking—what if you said, "Time for a new game! OK? Everybody jump under the parachute here for a second; we'll have somebody look out through the hole in the center of the parachute and be our driver and direct us on how to walk over to the middle of the basketball court." When you get to the middle of the basketball court, say, "Well, we need to put the parachute away before we get into the next game, so let's have everybody grab the edge of the parachute and, on the count of three, roll it up as fast as you can and see who can get to the middle of the chute first." Within 20 seconds you'll have your entire chute rolled up, probably better than you have ever rolled it up by yourself, and it will be really easy to stuff into the bag. Just by giving people focal points and some guidelines, you have them turn almost anything they are doing into a game that will be fun to play.

Other ways to fill the spaces between games in fun ways are to use chants or rituals. People can chant a sound or perform a ritual, such as silently showing the Rock, the Paper, or the Scissors while walking to a new area. Or they can silently hold up one finger, two fingers, a left hand or a right hand as they mill around to find other members holding up the same configuration. Maybe you are changing to a game that requires laying out some boundaries. Just before you lay out the boundaries say to people, "What I would like you to do is find a partner and, when you find that partner, explain to each other what your favorite dessert is and why it's your favorite dessert." By the time they have finished talking about this, you'll have time to set the boundaries and they will have done something fun and interesting. In addition, by just asking one partner to go on one side of the play area and one partner to go to the other side of the play area, you'll have divided up into two equally sized teams. So there you have it: Big Fun! Be sure to see Chapter 9, *A Bigger Bag of Tricks*, for more transition activities.

The idea in creating Big Fun is not only to make the high points high, but to keep the low points from being too low and to avoid letting the flow of fun turn into a trickle. So keeping the fun more or less constant becomes another element in making the middle part of a game work well.

Summary

The midgame takes you from the interest and intrigue of the presentation to the fulfillment of closure. During the midgame, be it a single game or a sequence of games in a play session, several things happen. One, there's a flattening of the hierarchy as the players' leader roles begin to emerge and there is also a shift in the original leader role which goes from high-visibility director to low-visibility supporter–facilitator. Two, a play community begins to evolve among the players, where they start to take ownership of the game and become empowered. Three, empowerment leads to creativity, multiplicity of input and game change.

As a leader, during the midgame, remember these three things:

1. *Maintain Safety*. Look for ways to maintain and increase the psychological and physical safety of individuals and the group as a whole.

2. *Maintain Interest and Enthusiasm*. Balance all the factors—high visibility, low visibility; safety, risk, challenge; excitement, boredom; anxiety; group empowerment, individual empowerment. Work as the balancing point to keep all the factors in dynamic tension. This creates excitement and interest.

3. *Maintain Flexibility*. Be open to change. Be open to stability. Be open to newness. Be open to doing the same thing over and over again. Just be open. Be ready to accept what the people in the group offer and what the universe offers in terms of opportunities. If you're willing to accept what the universe offers you, then you'll be able to navigate the whitewater, wherever it happens to be. You'll be able to go with the Flow. And you'll have a good time, rollin' on the river.

Chapter 5

Ending It All Well

All's well that ends well.

—William Shakespeare

Kill it before it dies.

—Joe Bob Briggs

Ending the Game or Games Session

Quick quiz: The best most exciting way to end a game is

   a. Have everyone get in a circle and close their eyes—then you leave the room.

   b. Have everyone stand 20 feet from the rim of the Grand Canyon facing the edge then close their eyes and run as fast as they can in a 30-foot race.

   c. Say, "That's it—I'm outta here!"

   d. Have everyone give themselves a rousing round of applause for playing well together.

If you said *d,* you are well on your way to discovering some of the best ways to end a game. If you said *b,* you are well on your way to San Quentin. And if you said *a* or *c,* you are just well on your way.

   The reason(s) why you want to end a game or games session well is (are)

   a. You don't want the positive emotional experience that you've provided for people to fall flat.

   b. You want to positively reinforce playing safely and playing well together.

   c. You want people to not get too tired and possibly injured.

   d. You want to leave people feeling that they want just a little bit more so they will come back again next time.

   e. All of the above.

If you answered *e* for this question, you most likely answered *d* for the previous question and show high levels of intelligence and sensitivity (of course).

In Chapter 3, *Getting It Going*, we emphasized how a well-led game is like a well-written novel or well-delivered speech. You have a good beginning, an exciting middle (with a lot of flow), and a meaningful, upbeat ending. Play is a qualitative, emotional experience and it's important that people leave a game or games session feeling good, and that they have emotional closure. That is what makes a good ending so important. If you can't "leave 'em laughing," at least "leave 'em glowing" (and smiling).

Timing

In comedy, life, and games leadership, timing is *almost* everything. When and why should you end a game? The answer to this lies in your sensitivity to the group you are playing with. You have to learn to read the group:

1. Has the activity run its course? Is it time to close, adapt the game for "re-arousal," or move on to another game?

2. What about nonverbal signals? Are people yawning, just going through the motions, getting hostile? Are there 100 people standing on the sidelines and only 6 people still left playing the game?

3. As a player–referee (participant), how are you feeling? Have you played a whole lot of theater–expressive type games and are close to being "expressed out?" How you're feeling as a player will be one good clue to the group's emotional or physical state. Not the only one, but something you should pay attention to. Do people need more of a competitive type of experience or perhaps a more quiet type of experience? Or maybe we all need a drink of water, a rest, or a nap.

4. Check once again for bellwethers, lightning rods, and superstars—almost every group has these. Sometimes they are the same person; sometimes they are different folks. Are you paying attention to them? Their actions will often tell you whether it's time to end a game. Bellwethers are people who are usually the first ones to start to get antsy or get a sense that it's time to change. They usually "act that out" by working their way over to the sidelines and sitting down, participating less enthusiastically, or even starting to be critical and counterproductive, risqué, dangerous (or sometimes obnoxious) in their play. This usually means that the game is boring or frustrating for them (or they are just plain tired).

   Lightning rods or superstars are also good group dynamic indicators. They are the highly energized "go for it" folks. If you're playing a theater game, they are the ones who put out the strongest or craziest emotions; if you're playing a competitive game, they are the ones who are going "full tilt—open throttle!" They are the ones by their energy and/or humor who are often helping set the tone for the group. They stand out. If they are not giving it 110%, that might be a signal for change or closure.

5. Last, one of the best (and most often overlooked) ways to know if it's time to end is simply to *ask*. How are you guys and gals doing? Are you pooped? Shall we keep going with this game? Is it time for a modification or a new game? When asking if we should continue, note the tone and energy of the response. If it's weak or "I think so..." then it's usually time for a change. If everyone's hand goes up really fast with a smile on their face, play on! By asking people, you're paying attention to their energies and natural rhythms and *empowering them* to define their own inner sense of "playtime boundaries." It may also be that half the people want to continue and the other half want a new game. This is a great opportunity to subdivide the group.

Clock Time

Only five minutes left before they shut off the lights and kick us out. Besides inner timing, there is another type of timing that we need to pay attention to when closing a game or games session: externally imposed time that comes from programmatic design or facility constraints. You have to end at eight o'clock. How do you handle it? Remember you've worked very hard to create this positive emotional experience for folks and you don't want the door slammed in their face, or to end in the dark! There is nothing worse than being in the middle of a laughing, rousing, connecting wonderful game and the leader abruptly says, "OK, it's time to go!" It's like pulling the plug (aaugh!?!) and a loss of emotional experience and closure results. Don't let it happen! So what can you do:

1. First, plan how and when you'll end before beginning. Look at your timing and game choice or sequence and what method you'll use to "close." Plan flexibly so you can have positive closure.

2 Don't start a new game when you're close to quitting time. It's better to end a bit early and maintain the positive feeling of the group.

3. Set folks up psychologically for the ending so it's not so abrupt. Say things like, "This will be the last two rounds" or "This will be

the last game of today's session" or "There'll be three more people who'll crawl on the Earthball and then we've got to close it down..."

4. End at a "natural" upbeat place (e.g., after a great play or move, or after a particularly funny remark—something that is not likely to be "topped" in the next five minutes).

5. There are really only three mistakes you can make when ending a game:

    a. ending too soon (i.e., cutting off the energy, feeling, too early)

    b. ending too late (i.e., the game is a plodding, stumbling, dying beast)

    c. ending without finesse, style, class, and pizzazz, or a combination of them (e.g., pizzazzy finesse; this one will cost you points in the hereafter).

So, in ending a game, honor the Flow and emotional experience so each of us can appreciate individually and collectively what we've shared.

Understanding the Game Life Span

The Play Interest Graphic Simulation (PIGS) arousal curve was developed with the support of the (Fred) Sanford Research Institute based on years of study of what happens every time you lead a game or play experience. At the beginning (or as we like to say, start) of the game(s) people are kind of coming in and they are "starting" to get aroused (excited) and the arousal curve is going up and it gets to its peak (Big Fun) and then plateaus a little bit and maybe then you do a little game change and maybe the curve climbs back up a bit and people are still having some pretty good fun. But then something starts to happen. The curve (and thus the pretty good fun) starts to go downhill (sometimes slowly, sometimes rapidly, but nevertheless down). So as a leader you need to pay attention to the arousal curve if you are to end the game with style and finesse. Here are a few implications and applications of PIGS:

1. Oink

2. Bacon

3. Heart disease

These first three were just to check if you're reading carefully.

4. Kill it before it dies. Games have a life span, so stop the game when folks are having a great experience, before they get bored, burnt out, or hurt.

5. Don't end too far downhill where the players forget how much fun it was at the peak. That's like flat seltzer. End on an *up note* (while it's still bubbly) and while the experience is still in the fun zone.

6. Apply the "one bite of the donut" theory. In other words leave them wanting just a little more. They will remember the thrills and excitement so that next time you suggest the same game they will say, "Yeah!" *People do remember.*

7. Your decision on when to end is directly related to *safety* (one of our fundamentals). Don't let your games get to where people are physically or emotionally burned out. Tiredness leads to lack of focus and sometimes to *injury* (to the spirit and/or to the body). When a game goes too far down the arousal curve that is when people turn ankles, twist knees, or just get a bad case of the "blahs." And that is not where we want to leave them.

Your judgment call of when to end, when to "re-arouse" by initiating some game change and when to start a new game involves very important decisions for you as a sensitive leader.

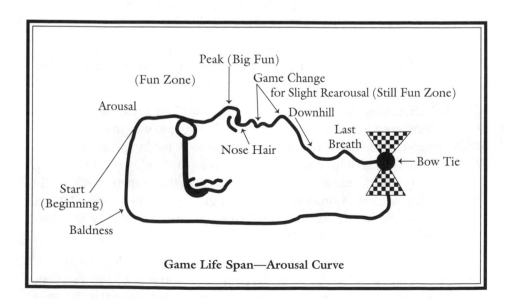

Game Life Span—Arousal Curve

Multiple Games Sessions and Other Miscellaneous Stuff

Before sharing with you some cheap tricks for ending games and some games and game-like activities that lend themselves to positive closure, we would like to mention a few additional principles to pay attention to when ending a series of games and a few other thoughts that don't seem to fit anywhere else:

1. In a games series it's often good to taper down the energy and end with a more quiet, focused game activity (especially with kids who may be going back into a classroom or getting on a bus—the bus driver will thank you).

2. One nice way to accomplish this with children (and adults for that matter) is to ask them to think of a quiet special place and to focus on rhythmic deep breathing. You can also take them on a guided visualization and have them imagine they are floating on a billowing cloud on a warm sunshiny day.

3. After a combative or highly competitive game with a bit of an *us versus them* component (even if it's very caring), it is always nice to end with an activity that brings us all together in some cooperative and/or connective way. It affirms that we all played well together. After all, that is what we really want to do at the end of any game or games session. *We want to positively reinforce that we played well together, played safely and supportively, and played caringly.* And you better believe that positive reinforcement works. It increases positive behavior. Have an M&M.

4. Smiling, eye contact and physical connection (e.g., hand-holding or shoulder-to-shoulder circles) are nice ways to reinforce and celebrate the positive "play community" that you've just shared.

5. Networking and exchanging "no obligation" addresses and phone numbers at the end of a play session is a simple way to extend the play community. This can be easily done by having people (optionally) sign a list during a natural break in the play session. Play ers (having made an initial connection) can then support each other's future efforts and play offerings (e.g., if I'm having a family picnic for my school, I could call you up and invite you to come help lead games with me).

6. Last, upon leaving a play session, please empower folks to help cooperatively load up all of the equipment and pick up trash so that we leave the play area in a cleaner condition at the end than when

we started. This also reinforces our strong connection with the earth. At the end of our family festivals we have everyone line up shoulder-to-shoulder at the edge of the playing field and walk the entire area picking up any trash. It is a powerful closure message. It also gets cleanup done quickly.

Some Games and Game-Like Activities That Lend Themselves to Good Endings

We found that some activities by their very nature tend to add a nice closure. They tend to be circular, reinforce physical connection, "achievement," co-operation, and communication *or* they tend to start small, in pairs, and get cumulative and connective so we're all one big group at the end. More specific directions for each can be found in the *New Games* and *Project Adventure* books (and many other sources), but don't be limited to these. Make up your own.

The Lap Sit

This ends with everyone sitting in a self-supportive circle on each others' laps. Prior to sitting on the lap of the person behind you in the circle (legs closed), it's a nice touch (pun intended) to have everyone close enough together in the circle (stepping inward, left hand facing the inside of the circle) to be able to massage the shoulders of the person in front of you. And then, since "turn about" is fair play, do an about face and massage the shoulders of the person who just massaged you.

Spirals

Spirals happen when we're holding hands in a big long line. We start with a couple of people at one end of the line curling in just a little bit to begin a spiral shape and the rest of the group, with a singing ritual like "Dear Friends" or "Happy Trails," walks around very, very slowly so we gradually develop a spiral formation. Imagine a snail shell, where the line begins to wind around itself. You have a series of concentric circles, with some people more towards the center of the clump, and some people, as the line ends, more toward the outside. At the end of your Spiral, you can give yourselves a nice hug, and maybe even create a "cave" for the innermost person to exit by taking with him or her the wound-up line so that you are unwinding from the middle outward.

5 $\frac{1}{2}$ (or More) Cheap Tricks to End a Game or Play Session

1. ***End With a "Rich You All."*** Rituals are wonderful ways to end a play session. They are used all the time at campfire closings. Remember singing "Day Is Done"? Invent your own rituals that symbolize and reaffirm how well you've played together. Maybe it's a quiet ritual like two long lines facing each other and doing a Japanese bow or perhaps a caring hug with the person facing you.

   Or maybe it's a wild and crazy ritual like a series of "high-fives" or "booty bumps" or maybe you make up a funny chant "May the *Farce* be with you"—and...

2. ***End in a Circle***. Circles, with hands on the shoulder of the person next to you, provides eye contact and body contact. You can see and feel the power and synergy of the group (it's bigger than all of us). It is especially important that the circle be facing inward. It helps to facilitate eye contact—although we're sure some great closing rituals could be invented with you facing outwards. If you do find yourself facing outwards, try bending over and looking through your legs to say good-bye (but make it quick, as people soon will begin passing out).

3. ***Use Huggles (Versus Huggies) and Pats on the Back***. Good circles (with your hands on the shoulders of the people next to you) naturally can progress into a huggle, a combination of a hug and a huddle. All it takes is a little step and then a squeeze. Umm...feels good! Everyone needs to give and get their daily quota of hugs.

   Another approach while everyone is in a hands on shoulders circle is to ask everyone to lift their hands slightly off the shoulders of the persons next to them and down lightly, higher up and down again. Then say, "Give yourselves a pat on the back," and have people keep patting each other!

4. ***End With a Song***. Again a circular formation works best. Keep it simple. A few suggestions:

   - "Happy trails to you until we meet again. Happy trails... Trails to you keep smiling until then..."

   - "Row, Row, Row Your Boat."

   - The Sufi song "Dear Friend"—"Dear Friend, Dear Friend, Can I tell you how I feel...You have given me your riches... And I love you so..." (Sung to "Rose Rose Rose Rose Red.")

---

5 $\frac{1}{2}$ (or More) Cheap Tricks to End a Game or Play Session (continued)

- "Happiness Runs" (in a circular motion) by Donovan (look it up; it's on the albums *Barabajagal* and *Troubadour: The Definitive Collection 1964–1976)—*A great closer.

- "The More We Play Together"—"The more we play to- gether together together...The more we play together the happier we'll be...'cause your friends are my friends and my friends are your friends...the more we play together the happier we'll be." (If you can't remember the tune make one up.)

- All of these can be sung as rounds which makes for a nice quiet spiritual ending. Or if people don't know the words, have them hum or whistle which usually makes for a pro- foundly silly ending (also OK).

5. *End With a Magic Circle*. End with people's hands on each others shoulders shuffle sliding to the right. Anyone who says, "Stop," has to put out a good wish for the group or an affirmation of something that he or she learned in the session.

6. *End With the Creation of the Universe* (otherwise known as the football cheer). Everyone's hands are in the circle...we start low with a low hum and build to the Big Bang! HmmmmMMMMM! Go!

7. *End by Applauding Each Others' Efforts*. "Give yourself a hand." "Good job." There are many goofy variations of applauding ones efforts (e.g., holding up a big hand—giv- ing yourself a hand, the fish shake, the lumberjack shake, and the round of applause).

8. *Create Your Own Ending*. Serious, silly, spiritual, seren- dipitous, or any other word that begins with *S* (OK, you can use the whole alphabet if you have to). But do some thing that positively reinforces playing well, caringly and safely.

Progressive Circles

Suppose two people were holding hands and they tilted their arms and rounded them out. We bet it would look like an *O*. And we'll bet every time they tilted it, it would make an "oooooo" sound. Suppose we got four people together holding hands. And when they lowered their hands they were very quiet but when they raised them we could hear a louder and deeper "oooooo!"

Suppose there were 8 folks or 16 or 32 or 64 or 512, all raising and lowering their arms in the "ooo" chant. Suppose we made a wave (like at a football game). Suppose we ended up with one last rousing "oooooo" and then were quiet. This is a Progressive Circle.

Get Down

Get Down is another of those games that starts with two folks in the center of a circle doing a movement—singing ritual—then cumulatively inviting more and more folks until the energy blows the roof off. Everyone ends up in the middle at the end going, "Up (chick-a-boom, chick-a-boom)...Down (chick-a-boom, chick-a-boom)...To the left ...To the right..." and really getting down!

Pruie

Pruie is another one of those cumulative games, only in this case it is an eyes-closed-searching-for-truth (the original Pruie) game. When you find the Pruie you can open your eyes and delight with all of your attached successful seekers in watching others attempting to find truth. At the end we're all connected and (semi) enlightened.

Magic Ball or Magic Pine Cone (Outdoor Version)

A somewhat more focused, profound, spiritual, or reflective way to end a series of games (when it's appropriate), is to have everybody in a seated circle and to pass an object around the circle (e.g., a Nerf ball or pine cone). As people receive the object, they can tell what the play session meant to them in terms of feelings, humor, fun, connection, insights. Other people in the circle can recognize that the experiences they were feeling were both unique and being felt by many other people as well. This can be a very moving ending (or at the very least affirmative of our shared experience). It's good to use a magic object like a Nerf ball that "allows" 30 to 60 seconds of sharing (or one breath of sharing) depending on the size of the group. This way it stays crisp and focused and doesn't drag on indefinitely.

Some Final Final Thoughts

We hope by now you get a sense of the importance of positive closure and not letting a game or games session go flat. End strongly and positively and people will remember.

One Final Game

If you want a really irreverent, foolish and funny way to end a game, or a series of games, you can get everybody together and say, "Everybody who really feels great about this play session say 'Yeah,'" and let them really cheer! Of course, there are going to be a lot of people who aren't cheering. So then you say, "Everybody who really *didn't* feel that great about the play session, say 'Yeah'!" And then, just to make sure you have everybody, say, "And now everybody who either felt really great or didn't feel great, say 'Yeah'!" We guarantee if you carry this off with a lot of love, care, enthusiasm, and zaniness, everybody will be cheering rabidly by the end of your play session.

Everyone who feels great that this chapter is over say, "Yeah!"

Chapter 6

On Games

Time is a child playing, moving counters on a game board; the King-dom belongs to the child.

—Heraclitus

Games Storm I

In the next 4 minutes and 22 seconds, brainstorm and write down the names of all the games you know. (If you finish in less than 4 minutes and 22 seconds, then you obviously don't know enough games, go out and learn a few. If it takes you more than 4 minutes and 22 seconds then you can have extra time.)

Games Storm II

In the next 2 minutes and 11 seconds (you should be twice as fast because of your warmup) write down what you believe to be key concepts or principles related to good games (e.g., inclusive, promotes teamwork, flexible, fun) whether they be simple or complex.

Why Games? Why Not Just Play?

We've emphasized the importance of play and the role of the play leader in facilitating high states of playfulness. Now we want to look at the "tools," over and above facilitation skills, that the leader has to work with. We want to look at games.

We define games as "a structured way to play" (*of course,* there are other structured ways to play). This statement has two meanings. First, it means that the way in which we play is structured, there are boundaries, so there are things we do and things we don't do. Because of this structure we all play the same way and we know if we come back to play the game next week the rules will be the same. By having structure we also have freedom to be creative within the structure. Second, it means that the game provides a structured manner in which to achieve the "play experience." It's like a well-worn path—we feel like if we follow it (with the right attitude and facilitation), we can be pretty sure that we'll find that quality we call play.

"Free" play is more like untracked territory. Free play is often experimental, an adventure. Sometimes we find great new things and sometimes we just wander around. Open-ended free play is developmentally and creatively important, but oftentimes we want to revisit a certain pattern of fun. Games are one way to retain the predictable pattern from some of our best play experiences (or explore elaborated versions of it). Check out how many games have elements of tag in them (baseball, football, Parcheesi, and many more).

Games are like a skeleton, a framework that supports the muscles and organs and allows the life blood of play to flow through and keep the organism alive. In fact, a game is similar to a living organism in that it is a dynamic system with various interrelated parts. If all these parts are in proper balance then we'll likely experience play through the game.

So what makes for a good game? Three qualities to look for are

!   *Attractiveness*. The kind of excitement that draws you to a game, that makes you want to get involved and give it a try.

!! *Accessibility*. Openness to participation by as many and as varied a group of people as possible, without a lot of restrictions or barriers so that ideally, anyone who wants to play can play.

!!! *Simplicity–Complexity*. A combination of simplicity (easily understood rules) and the possibility of complexity (of strategies, of variations).

Now obviously not every good game is going to be attractive to everybody. Different people will like different things. And, some good games are not very accessible. Take ice hockey for instance. It's generally only available to people with access to equipment who skate pretty well and even then, for the most part, only during a certain time of the year and in a certain part of the country. Still, for some people, hockey is so attractive that they will go long distances or stay up to rent a rink for a 3 a.m. game. For others, hockey becomes accessible by playing on inline skates or in street shoes with a ball instead of a puck. For many people, hockey only becomes accessible to them as spectators watching others play.

The important point is that, whatever the game, if it's not attractive (aka, fun) people won't want to play it. If it isn't accessible in some way, they won't be able to play it. And if it doesn't offer the possibility of ongoing challenge and fun, they won't return to it (think of the ongoing appeal of games like Monopoly and chess). Especially for mass participation, it's important to look for games that are easy to learn, have low organization, have minimal equipment requirements and can be played almost anywhere by most people. *And that are fun*. Think about the games that you know. On a scale of 1 to 10, score them for attractiveness, accessibility, and simplicity–complexity.

Types of Games Bonus Points Exercise!

1. In 10 minutes write down all the different types of games you can think of (e.g., board, guessing, word, ball, tag games). Scoring: 1 point for each 2 games up to 20 and 1 point for each game over 30.

2. Score 1 bonus point for each game from the game storm exercise that you can fit into a category.

3. Score 2 bonus points for giving attractiveness, accessibility, and simplicity–complexity ratings to each game on a 1 to 10 scale.

4. Go!

"Flavors" of Games

If games are tools, there are many accepted systems of classifying those tools: by equipment (e.g., ball, word, or tag games), by location (e.g., board, field, or water games), by the players (e.g., small group, large group, children's, or adult games), by energy level (e.g., active, quiet, or sit down games), and many other common categories that you could make up. It's probably most important that you develop a system of classification that works for you—a workable games list with the titles of games you know grouped appropriately. It is also worthwhile to familiarize yourself with some of the other common systems by observing the way game books are organized. For your personal edification, and ours, here's how we do it.

The Bill System

- Openers—icebreaker mixer-types

- Combative—active and more aggressive in nature

- Expressive—theater-type games

- Trust—games that build trust and interaction

- Tag-Type Games—you're it

- Group Builders—challenge, adventure, and initiatives

- Quiet and Guessive—you guessed it

- Games That Teens Like—sure winners for those who sometimes appear to know it all and/or want an extra challenge

- Games for Munchkins—winners for the littlest ones

- Games for Small Groups (eight or less)

- Games for Mixed Age Groups

- Sport-Like Activities—like Frisbee Baseball

The John System

- Trust—activities that inspire contact, friendly interaction, cooperation, initiative, emotional safety and trust

- Soft War—competitive even combative types of games, almost always win–lose

- Creative Play—games that call more on the imagination and the intellect, such as theater games and word games

Each of these categories are subdivided into high-, medium- and low-intensity levels. Thus a low-intensity Soft War game like Word War can be selected when a group needs to let off steam but it isn't the right time or place for a physical game. Each of our games lists (in their entirety) can fit on one to three five-by-eight cards.

In both the Bill and John systems of game classification, there is an emphasis on the feelings or qualities of the game, what we call *flavors*. The leader's role is to assess what flavor the group is hungry for. Your games list system helps you find an appropriate game in a timely manner once you determine what flavor you want. It also helps you think on your feet when 78 wild-eyed kindergartners are attacking you, saying, "We wanna play!" The more you lead games, the better your taste buds get at sensing the right flavor at any given time.

All this talk about flavor, makes us think about food, which leads us to the Chinese Restaurant Model of play leadership. (Nice segue, huh?)

Game Segues

You know how when you look at the menu in a Chinese restaurant, everything is nicely classified—Appetizers, Soups, Chicken, Pork, Beef, Seafood, Noodles, Vegetarian—and the spicy dishes are marked with a little red pepper symbol? Your games list is like the restaurant menu. How you choose the dishes and the order in which you play them is what we call *segueing,* the transition from one segment to another.

Segues and sequencing are very important in using games as tools to create play. You may want to select a series of games that mixes and balances the flavors, like selecting one dish from each category, with one out of four being spicy. Or for a really hot group you might pick all spicy dishes.

For the best effect, you usually want to plan out the play session, the way you would plan out the menu for a very special dinner. To do this you want to think about what kind of experience you want to create for the players and plan accordingly. This brings us back to thinking about what kind of experience our players want, which is what is most important. We want to make sure that once we know or think we know what kind of experience our players want, our games list menu is set up in such a way that we can organize and create that experience. Remember, "form follows function!"

Using Games I

There are at least 297 important questions to be asked about using games, however we'll only ask three of them here: where, when, and why. The other 294 questions will have to wait until we finish playing.

For the last few hundred years, most games and play have been considered frivolous and generally restricted in use, mostly to kids, on the playground, and after school or chores were finished. Today that seems to be changing (at least somewhat). Games are starting to be recognized as tools with uses that are more significant than frivolous. And even frivolity is being recognized as useful. Games are used by youngsters and adults as learning tools to explore new areas and to practice skills. Games and play are also used as a way of building community in businesses (team-building and laughter and humor in the workplace as stress reducers), schools, and cities (community development programs).

In some circles a revolution is going on in which the divisions between work and play are breaking down. Work can be organized to make it more fun and play can be organized to make it more developmental. And, as we know, even nonutilitarian, free play, and frivolity have many benefits.

We would encourage you as a playmaker and leader to look for ways to stretch the boundaries of where, when, and why to use games. Make the way you use games a game in itself—get creative. Look at ways to use games at work—to kick off the day, for an energy break, to celebrate, at conferences and retreats, for team-building and training. And, be creative about working more play and games into your nonwork lives for fun, friendship, personal growth and adventure.

What happens as we become more adept players is that we recognize the possibilities for play in almost any situation, in every place we go and in (almost) all the things we do. As playmakers we can start to open people up to the possibility that life really can be a successful and joyful game. Challenge yourself to bring a smile to the face of a bored shopkeeper or to get people on the bus laughing (a singing game?) or to turn a problem at work into a puzzle to be solved by playing together. The only limits to the use of games and play are our imaginations and our willingness to go for it.

So, like, do it dude(tte)!

Using Games II: Just When You Thought It Was Safe to Play (Game Change and Invention)

For most of this book we've written about *how* to use games. Still, there is more to be said. Well, enough said about that.

In talking about how to use games, we need to discuss a central concept we call "the living game." What we mean is that a game has a sort of life to it, that it can grow and change, adapt to circumstances, such as players and the environment. Games are processes more than products, verbs more than nouns, dynamic more than static. Of course, to change and grow, games need help. That is where we come in. As playmakers we have to be open to development, to the changes that will keep the game exciting for the participants (i.e., attractive and accessible).

The practical application of the philosophical concept of the living game is called Game Change. There are 4.5 types of game change: variation, combination, adaptation, and innovation. Innovation deserves 1.5 points because it's more than change, it's creation!

Variation

Variation is pretty simple. We start off with basic tag, one "it" and lots of "not its." Then someone suggests that when you're tagged you become frozen and we have Freeze Tag. Someone else suggests that everyone have the power to freeze and the challenge to be the last one left unfrozen, and we have Everybody Is It Tag. Then in a wild leap of imagination, someone suggests that there be only one "not it" and that everyone else try and catch the "not it" and to be clear on who the "not it" is, we have the "not it" carry something, like a ball and sure enough you have your basic game of Fumbles. Now as most of us can imagine, Fumble is only a few predictable variations away from football.

A few basic principles of game change that apply to variation include the following:

1. ***KISS***. Keep It Splendidly Simple. In other words don't try to change too many things at once.

2. ***Try It***. The death of many a potentially good game concept is the "Oh, that won't work" reptile-brain thinking of many heart dead intellectuals. You can spend hours arguing about what people think will or won't work and get really depressed. Or you can get elated by spending hours playing with different variations and know what works and what doesn't. Most of the time you'll find that you have a great time even if you find that none of the ideas that came up "worked." Get out of your head and get "moving."

3. ***Name It***. Making up names for games is a lot like song writing. It's always easier to write the title than the song. So make up names for different variations because it's fun and it helps you keep track of them.

Combination

Combination is a little more complicated than variation. It is more like moving in with someone compared to going on a date. It usually involves numerous changes to both games and it often involves unanticipated surprises. (Have you ever had an anticipated surprise? Was it still a surprise? It is a Zen kind of question.)

A good example of combining games is Rock, Paper, Scissors Tag. It started with the observation of a game called Lemonade, which involves miming out various jobs or trades and then one team chasing the other when it figures out what the trade being mimed is. Well the miming part seemed a little weak, but the chasing part seemed like fun and everyone always liked RPS, alias Ro-cham-beau, so why not put them together!

RPS Tag, originally named RPS+ (meaning augmented in the musical sense) has become a modern classic, wherein two teams of 5 to 500 huddle to decide which of the three symbols they will "throw" and then face off across a line of scrimmage and go through the ritual of chanting, "Rock, paper, scissors," as they show the different symbols. At the end of the ritual, the two teams simultaneously show their secret symbols and the team that wins chases the team that loses, capturing any players who are tagged before they reach a safety zone. The team that wins is the team that has all the players at the end and the team with no players left automatically loses. RPS+ has surprisingly, generated numerous alternate symbols such as, dynamite, water, thermonuclear war, and also variations including Giants, Elves, and Wizards, which is almost equally as popular.

Principles for combining games: Refer to *Try It* and *Name It* discussed earlier in this chapter, then keep *KISS* in mind as you make the necessary adjustments of integrating the best perceived elements of two (or more) games.

Adaptation

Adaptation presents its own set of challenges in that adaptation is usually a change that is forced by circumstances, for instance, the abilities of the players or the available space or equipment. Some may be relatively easy and some adaptations may be highly challenging or perhaps impossible. Wheelchair Basketball works very well, but Wheelchair RPS+ may be more complex (not impossible, but with significant safety considerations). The best advice on any adaptation is try it with the conditions with which you anticipate working. For example, the best way to find out what works with a person with a disability is to get that person involved in the game and have him or her contribute to the game development process. Ask him or her for his or her input in an appropriate way. It's as simple as that.

We once had a mixed group of folks both with and without disabilities playing together and someone suggested a game of Knots or Human Tangle. By trying various suggestions and continually checking on what worked for the players in wheelchairs, as well as the other folks, we eventually developed an adaptation with the players holding 6- to 10-foot pieces of rope that allowed everyone needed arm extensions. The chairs could then roll over or under the rope extensions. Hoop Circle Race is another good example. In the traditional game hand-holding circle teams attempt to pass a Hula-Hoop over everyone's body around the circle without letting go of hands. By using an 8- to 10-foot length of rope tied together in a circle (instead of a Hula-Hoop) the activity can include people in wheelchairs because the rope circle is large and flexible enough to pass over and under the chairs.

In many cases adaptations are needed to account for different ages and development levels, and it is very useful to look at ways to break a game down or build it up. The challenge of a game as simple as tick-tack-toe can be increased to adapt it for older children or adults by making more complex matrices and more markers in a row, such as Go Bang and Pente, or making it three dimensional, such as Score Four. Now those can be tough games.

The best principle for adapting games is to play the games with the people for whom you want the game to work and get them involved in the adaptation process. Let the players decide! Try for an appropriate match between the players' needs and abilities (what they *can* do—not what they can't do) and the modification of the key Elements of the Game. Use these elements to guide your adaptations and enjoy the process of creation and inclusion (which might just be a fun experience in and of itself).

Innovation

Innovation is a whole new ball game. We use the term to refer to the development of a new and completely different game form. As such, it doesn't happen very often. Innovation is both the easiest and the most difficult of game change operations. When you sit around and try and think up something completely new, it's pretty difficult to do. On the other foot, when an idea just pops into your head in a moment of inspiration, it's effortless!

Just such an event occurred one fine training day in Waterloo, Ontario, Canada. The room we were working in was L-shaped with a door at either end. Next to each door were four switches for the overhead lights. As I left after one session, I noted that the switches were all in the down position. Upon returning, through the other door, I observed that some of the switches were up and some were down. Very curious. The peculiarity of this situation led to some exploration and soon, two of us were madly flipping switches on and off at either end of the room to try and get all the lights on or off. We began scoring a point for a full dark or light. And thus, the moment of inspiration begat a game innovation, which begat numerous variations, which begat adaptations when other people began to arrive back in the room and wanted to get in on the game. We adapted a two-person game into a team game by having players lie on the floor and watch the light show until a point was scored, at which point (har har), the "switcher" switched with a watcher and the watcher became the new switcher. I don't know that we ever added the combination level to the process. However, I think a case can be made that after the blackout of the entire East Coast of North America about 20 minutes into the game (surely a coincidence) a number of other games such as Demolition Derby took place, giving us a sweep of the four types of game change—variation, combination, adaptation, innovation—in one fell swoop.

So, think about it. Is there another way to play the old games you've known for years. Is there a way to get your players involved in creatively developing new games. More than anything else, every futurist tells us that the future will be a time of change and the need for creativity and flexibility will be paramount. Learning to change the rules and make up new games will teach all of us essential mental and emotional survival skills, just as early games taught our ancestors physical survival skills. So, if you don't like the game, go out and make up a new one of your own!

Elements of Games

Just as games are tools for us to create play and to bring people together, each game has various parts we can change to create a new game. We refer to these parts as the *elements* of the game. Most of us know these elements from direct experience. Some of them may be described by different names by different people. Don't worry about it. We've included the absolutely authoritative "Bill and John List of Game Elements" that gives you all the right answers for any time the topic comes up in conversation. Feel free to change and/or adapt the list. Just make sure you have a good reason for doing it.

Being aware of the elements of games will also give you greater leverage in changing games and discussing what works and doesn't work in your new inventions. It will also allow you to do systematic and rigorous analysis of other people's games (should you ever wish to do so). Just remember a principle mentioned earlier—Keep It Splendidly Simple. Analyze or change one element at a time to see how it works and what its effect is on playability. You can also check out the *More New Games* invent a game grid and process if you like. Here's *our* list in no particular order that should be all you need for invention and adaptation:

- *Players*. The one indispensable element of any game (tell that to Deep Blue, the chess computer).

- *Goal*. The objective to be accomplished, as in "field goal," or the goal of the game. When the three pointer was added to basketball it really changed the strategy of the game.

- *Strategies*. Approaches to meeting the challenges and reaching the goal.

- *Challenge*. The obstacles in achieving the goal or level of efforts that it takes (either competitively or cooperatively).

- *Roles*. The parts that different players take on in the game such as "it" and "not it" or "pitcher" and "batter."

- *Action*. The basic form of engagement in the game (e.g., tag, capture, guess, solve).

- *Interaction*. The relations of players to each other and the group, such as player versus group or group versus player as in some guessing games, or group versus group, player versus player, team versus team, player versus team, or players versus monster (e.g., Godzilla).

- *Scoring*. System of gaining points toward the goal. What is rewarded and how it's rewarded.

- *Environment*. The place we play, the physical setting—inside, outside, soft surface, in the water, on a table.

- *Rules*. The "constraints" and/or agreements of play. There are a million of them.

- *Boundaries*. Space and time limitations. Changing the boundaries can have a dramatic impact on the game. How about a lacrosse field three-miles long and two-miles wide, a two-day "running" clock and no time-outs.

- *Equipment*. The materials we play with. How about volleyball with a six-foot diameter Earthball!

- *Movement*. The way we can move in the game (e.g., running, crawling, jumping, skipping) and the way we can move equipment (e.g., rolling, throwing). Could we tie a Nerf ball to a string and the other end to a wheelchair so we all could play ball tag and the ball could be easily retrieved? (What is the movement in a word game?)

- *Fantasy*. The imaginative context in which the game is played. It's Rock, Paper, Scissors versus Giants, Elves, Wizards versus Tiger, Hunter, Camera.

- *Ritual*. The little things we say and do to frame the game such as the coin toss, bowing, handshakes, group cheers, the skate by, and the net jump. Creating ritual can add to the humor or the seriousness of the game depending on what you do and how you do it.

- *"It" Power*. How much power does the individual or collective "it" have to be relatively "successful." If one "it" can't make the tags, can we go to two "its," or if it is too easy for "it" can we make "it" hop on one foot? We'll say more about this in Chapter 8, *Advanced Leadership Skills*.

- *Flavor*. The basic approach of the game such as competitive, cooperative, expressive, quiet...

There are probably a few dozen other elements that deserve mention, and you may want to continue to add to your own list. What is important is that the awareness of the elements of the game become a part of you as a leader. Awareness of them will give you power and flexibility to change the game well and this in turn will add to your success and the satisfaction of you and the other players. Which of course is what you want.

In review, a few tips on rules for changing games:

1. *Just Do It! Heuristically!* In other words, trial and error. Talking about ideas doesn't really get you very far. In ten minutes of trying it out you'll know more about what works and what doesn't than in ten hours of discussion.

2. *KISS*. As we said before, change a little at a time, go slow to fast, try one type of change and then see if you need another adjustment to make it even better. If you try to change everything at once you often end up with mush.

3. *Involve the Players!* More heads are better than one. Empower people to generate new ideas and test them out.

4. *????* Fill in the blank. As you become proficient at changing games keep track of what works for you and add it to your list.

End Game

As we end this solemn discourse on games, remember games are a way to reach the experience of play. Games are tools to create the work of art, they aren't the work of art itself. And it is also important to remember that games should be treated with respect like the tools of an artist or a craftsman. In some cases, like a fine tool, the tools themselves become artworks, and in fact some games can be that well-crafted.

Games need flexibility and stability, intrigue and predictability, balance and lopsidedness. These attributes plus quality are part of what makes them fun. But they are also whole systems containing the basic elements of life (e.g., rules, roles, interaction patterns, goals) and occasionally the best games become self-contained worlds unto themselves, if only for a moment.

Games are also symbolic. They are a vehicle for the freedom to play and be spontaneous and reach beyond the limiting rules of the "real" world. In another sense they are a symbol of the need for order and structure, for having a clear purpose and goals and defined roles and procedures. The interaction of this play–game can be a symbol of our creativity and vitality as a people and the cross-cultural nature of games holds great potential for building bridges and breaking barriers. How do we keep inventing the big game of peaceful, positive interaction?

Chapter 7

Events or the Big Game

Events are mostly easy if you know what you're doing.

—supposedly attributed to Bill Graham's mother, Martha

An event is just like a game only bigger.

—Bill and John

Before getting started with this chapter, take two minutes to make as many three or more letter words as you can with the letters contained in *events.* Ready? Go! How many did you come up with? Now cross off ones that we also had on our lists (Boggle rules!). We had "seven," "ten," and "nets." Now imagine that there were four other folks doing the same thing. Then imagine that there were 400 other people playing this events word game *and* a wide variety of *other* word games around tables, on rugs with big stuffed pillows, with different levels of competition or cooperative teamwork required—crossword freaks, password fanatics, kids, families, and people trying to learn how to spell. That is the difference between a game, a play session, and an event. An event is to a play session as a play session is to a single game. Bigger, more considerations, but most of the same basic principles that we've been talking about throughout this book still apply, particularly the four Ps in Chapter 3, *Getting It Going.*

Why Do It?

There are a variety of good reasons to do an event that often transcend what you accomplish in a smaller play session. Here are a few. We're sure you can think of more.

1. You can have a wider variety of games, play experiences, and types of people.

2. You can have greater visibility for your efforts. This can help spread the word about play to the average Joe and Jane on the street and perhaps give them permission to come join in and reconnect with their own playful spirit and with others.

3. You might make the evening news (especially if you send them a news release ahead of time).

4. It's a chance to establish and/or reaffirm a sense of community.

5. It's a chance to celebrate a theme (e.g., National Let's Dismantle Protestant Guilt Week, Peace Day, Family Fun Month, Earth Day).

6. It's a chance to reaffirm the value of active participation (doing) versus spectating (watching)...being a *creator* of your own fun versus being a passive consumer that needs to be "entertained."

7. An event provides more choices for people. Where there are more choices there is more freedom. Where there is more freedom there is a greater likelihood of playfulness and exploration.

8. We can reexperience and/or reaffirm the "human" bonds that tie us together, whether in a business setting, on a college campus, in a city with a multicultural population, in a family-oriented town, or with a group of folks, abled and (dis)abled, working on resocialization or integration issues.

9. We've a chance to celebrate and *value* differences rather than to "evaluate" them comparatively and hierarchically (you are smarter, I am taller, you are more athletic, I am a "spaz," you are a wimp).

10. We can affirm the *wellness* of playing *together*—both for individual and community mental health. The evidence is clear that Good Friends are Good Medicine and that people who are disconnected, disengaged, and/or isolated experience higher levels of physical and mental illness.

11. It's a chance to "bring people in"—in the name of fun—and educate them (with flyers, information booths) about other serious issues (community and family resources, child abuse, healthy kids, preventative services).

What This Chapter Will and Won't Do

What we *won't do* is walk you through all of the logistics, steps, timelines, committee responsibilities, and such that relate to doing an event. Each local situation will be different and there are several excellent "event operations manuals" (listed in Chapter 12, *Resources, Connections, and Beyond*) that will give you all of the checklists and tasks in simple layman's terms. So even if you've never done an event, these books will make it easy. The best of these is from the Canadian Parks and Recreation Association, *Fitnic—A Festival of Food Fun Family and Fitness*. Another great logistic tool is the *New Games Training Manual* (which is out of print but many copies are floating around the country with the 100,000-plus people who attended the early New Games Training).

What we *will do* is share with you stories, frameworks, principles, and personal insights from our combined 40-plus years of doing hundreds of different kinds of events around the world ranging in size from 50 folks to 60,000 people. Stuff that generally isn't written in the logistic books and that we found out in the school of hard knocks (and white socks). We believe that if you integrate these principles with strong logistics and planning, your event can't help but be a success.

The Song Remains the Same: The Fundamentals

If you want to pull off a good event, you have to come back to the same basics that were important for leading a good game: safety and enthusiasm. We'll keep coming back to this throughout the chapter. Just as you had an "internal" safety consciousness for each individual game you led, you must now have a consciousness of the safety of the entire festival and how the games relate to each other. This might include such things as choosing appropriate areas for certain activities so there is no conflict between activities, walking the field and inspecting the play area for any hazards and removing them, centralizing equipment, and creating "safe spaces" for people to enter and leave the games.

As far as enthusiasm is concerned, you want that same positive energy for life, for play, for community, for the "child within," that you had while leading a game. An energy that makes people want to say, "Yeah, I want to play!" You want a synergistic positive energy that comes from a motivated group of leaders who know a wide range of games and facilitation techniques. This energy will be infinitely contagious and the whole much bigger than the sum of the parts.

You also want to strive for this same level of enthusiasm as an organizer of the event—with the leaders, the media, your community and corporate sponsors, and your committee heads. Keep 'em excited!

What's Different?

Let's refer back to the *elements of play* discussed earlier in the book: the players, the situation, the setting, the games, and the leaders.

The Players

1. How do we address them and communicate with them? Do we need a megaphone, a P.A. system, or a sound or visual symbol that can get everyone's attention? Do the leaders need good signaling, focusing, or attention-getting devices?

2. Do we need to group them in some way so that we can be seen and heard (e.g., at the signal everyone sits on the chalk circle lines, or has his or her toes on the rope)? What other ways do we need to group them (e.g., by size of group, by size of people)? Does the group need to be subdivided and rotated every 20 minutes to a difference play station?

3. When you have more people you have a greater variety of folks (abled, disabled, parents, munchkins, teens, bosses, workers, "fit," "unfit," and athletic). Are there any things that you'll have to do to take this variety into account.

4. You may not have to do any of the above, but it's important that you ask the question, "Who are the players and what does this mean for the event?"

The Situation

1. What is the focus of the event (e.g., Family Fun Day, Red Ribbon Week, Founder's Day)?

2. Does the event stand on its own or is it part of a larger community event (e.g., our three-hour Pacifica 1,500-person Family Fun Fest is part of a citywide two-day 60,000-person Art, Food and Wine Festival). What is the relationship of the two? Do they feed into each other?

3. What is the overall purpose of the event (e.g., to show kids natural high, drug free alternatives; corporate team building)?

4. How is the situation in the general community (positive or divisive)? We've done events where the purpose of the fun festival was cultural and racial integration. Two weeks before the event there was a "riot" in the community and tensions were high. We've also done corporate team-building events where the atmosphere was filled with employee worries about layoffs. You can't always mitigate all of these but the point is you should be aware of them

and sensitive to them in your planning, preparation and training of leaders.

5. The point of all of this is to ask a lot of framing questions to context the situation and to avoid horror stories (or at least not have too many surprises). *You can never ask too much.* Here is an example:

We planned a college Spring Fling event in Southern California (where it never rains) for a small College of Arts and Crafts student body. We didn't anticipate the weather (it rained). So we didn't ask about the indoor alternative space, or what else was going on around or during the Spring Fling. When we arrived, we were ushered into a small, concrete, pillared indoor college building where 200 drunken students were jam packed in front of four, six-foot high disco speakers blaring "Saturday Night Fever." The floor was strewn with paper plates, cups, old chicken bones and *lots* of beer cans. The local event coordinator looked at us and said, "Here they are. Organize some games—that's what you were hired for!" It was a game leader's nightmare! Needless to say, we coped fairly well and pulled it off (I remember those empty cans bouncing on the parachute) but we learned a valuable lesson. *Ask. See the site* (ahead of time, if possible, or at least get there early on the day of the event). *Anticipate* and *assert your needs* (what *you need* to pull off a good event). Some questions to ask:

•   What is happening in the situation?

•   What kinds of food and drink are being served? (You need different planning for alcohol-related events.)

•   How will folks be dressed? (Can you predefine that?)

•   What is the entertainment (you could be competing with an amplified sing-along contest)?

•   Is there anything before, during, or after your event? Will people be racing to get into the chow line midway through your event?

•   What is the alternative indoor space? (Have people describe it to you very *specifically:* surface, size.) Who is next door? Can you be loud? Who is usually using the space? Are you kicking anybody out?

•   How is the event being publicized? (This helps shape the situation. Can you write the words? If not, send them key words and phrases (e.g., everyone welcome, win-win, family, team building).

We could write a whole book on situational "almost horror stories" and the questions to ask to almost avoid them. The key is to ask, to anticipate, to help define the situation favorably, and to still plan flexibly.

The Setting

1. Is the space safe? Are there hazards (obvious and "hidden ones")?

2. Are there a variety of spaces? Is there shade or sun? Are there quiet spaces? Is the space hard, soft, good for active games, sloped? Is it separated from the seating and eating areas? (If so, you'll have to figure out how to get them up and moving.)

3. Are there benches? Is there water and rest room access nearby? Is it an auditorium with rows of chairs? Are they locked in or can they be moved?

4. What is the level of maintenance: clean, no glass, floor swept, no dog doo-doo?

5. Does the environment say, *"let's play"*? In other words, is it inviting, visible, and accessible?

6. Does the park have a bad reputation and is there any counteractive publicity that you can do to overcome peoples fears of attending?

7. Are there other hazards that you need to work with (e.g., streets and cars?) We remember this beautiful setting near a lake that seemed ideal until some enthusiastic players pushed a 40-pound Earthball and some other players into the lake. Big Fun (unless of course one of them had accidentally drowned).

8. Once again, find out as much as you can about the *physical setting* you'll be operating in—ask very specific questions and help define the most safe, inviting, playful space that you can (and/or modify your plan appropriately).

The Games

1. The key thing to consider is that in events the size of games can vary greatly. We've had 300 people in a Lap Sit game and hundreds of people joining and leaving an ongoing game of Rock, Paper, Scissors. Sometimes big games can almost become events

in and of themselves. When things get big, you need enough leaders to keep it safe and fun—are you covered?

2. At events it's important to have a variety of games (e.g., active, quiet, sports-oriented, theater expressive-oriented) and enough of them going on simultaneously so that each participant can find something to his or her liking as he or she wanders in and out of activities.

3. The concept of "stations" is relevant here, whether they be permanent game stations (e.g., parachute games in one place, Earthball in another) where people rotate freely or on a set time schedule (many elementary school festivals work this way) or they be *amorphous ever-changing* "stations" where you have several leaders in different "areas" and a parachute game might magically transform into a series of other circle-type games. This model tends to be more responsive to participants' changing needs versus a preset structure.

The Leaders

1. Remember to reinforce the leadership principles in earlier chapters of this book (especially the *fun*damentals).

2. Proper training for leaders is essential (both general and "event specific" skills). The bigger the event the more extensive the training, both in terms of safety and fun facilitation.

3. Proper leader–participant ratios ensure a safe, fun, engaging community building event. Your ratio will vary depending on the nature of the activity. In Pacifica's "very active" 1,500-person Family Fun Fest, we had over 50 trained leaders and sometimes even then we were stretched a little thin.

4. Leaders need to be coordinated and trained to have both *meta-* (within the game they are leading or helping lead) and *mega-* (their place within the entire festival) *consciousness*. That is, on the *meta* level, suppose you're playing or helping a fellow leader with a parachute game, and you can see that he is running out of ideas. You can consult your games list (you did bring it!? If not, reread Chapter 6, *On Games*) and perhaps even huddle with a fellow leader to be ready with a compilation of ideas for follow-up circle games. At the *mega*-event level, suppose you looked up and saw

there was only one leader leading parachute games and there were six leaders helping with the Earthball. You might go over or suggest that a couple of your team members go over to the chute and help out. Or suppose you looked up and saw that there were five parachute games going on or five very active games. You might take it upon yourself to start a quiet game so there would at least be some choices for the participants who were "shopping" (and didn't want to buy "active").

A Few Additional Notes on Orchestration and Sideline (Peripheral) Activities and Logistics

At events the concept of orchestration also becomes important. The placement of certain games is important so that active games do not conflict with quiet ones. There is nothing worse than playing a guessing game and living with the paranoia that you'll be crushed by a runaway Earthball. Also, at most of our events we insist that there be no amplified music. It tends to dominate the space and leaders can't peacefully communicate with the players.

We've found that at big play events it helps to have at least a few peripheral activities around the "sidelines" of the field where the game stations are located. These might include such things as face painting, stilts, giant bubbles, scrap crafts, giant mural painting, origami, boffer (foam swatter) circles, and board games tables. There are good reasons for this:

1. They provide a psychologically safe entree into the play festival. A person might not immediately want to join a game, but might paint a face or catch a Frisbee. Kind of like sticking a foot in the water to test it.

2. They provide for more quiet "time-out" spaces.

3. They are an area that can refocus the energy to artistic expression, exploration, and other flavors.

The logistical aspects of a festival require tireless and relentless attention to the details behind the scenes. These are the checklists that get done by a timeline that no one sees or appreciates (however, if things are forgotten they are in fact noticed). Refer to the excellent logistics books that are available and modify according to your local needs. There are always a lot of little things on the day of the event that are needed (e.g., hammers, nails, scissors, water, tables, chairs, parking, extra keys, stakes for signs). There is nothing worse than running around a couple of hours before 1,000 people are to arrive trying to find a stapler or a hammer to pound the stakes for your signage. *Pay attention to detail—write it down.* Have a year-round event development checklist broken down by committee, and a week before the event checklist and a day of the event checklist (including all equipment supplies and materials needed). Believe it or not, proper logistics handling helps to create the proper atmosphere of freedom, playfulness, and exploration.

Some Notes on the Process of Large Event Development

Planning

1. Bucky Fuller once said, "Defining the 'problem' is 75% of realizing the solution." Clearly defining your vision of the event goes a long way toward making it happen. Then you can effectively develop your plan of action organization and your timeline.

2. Thinking early on about how you're going to spread the work load and get a "buy-in" for the event will save you a lot of grief in the long run. The planning of the event can actually be a miniature model of how you create and reinforce community.

Preparation

1. Who and where are your human resources for the event, such as community organization leaders, games leaders, peripheral activity folks such as artists and mothers, food booth people, and committed workers? Who can do the lead-up and day-of-event tasks?

2. What and where are your nonhuman resources (e.g., money, materials, donations, bartered goods or in-kind services)? (We've had local carpenters make all of our stilts and a furniture store save cardboard boxes for us for a year for our "cardboard city.")

3. Pay particular attention to how you can continue to motivate and enthuse your "team" (committee members). It might be by bringing treats to the meetings or by playing a short game to start each meeting or by showing last year's slides. You want to keep that behind-the-scene energy building right through to the day of the event.

Publicity

1. This needs to be well thought out. What are the most effective community information vehicles? Publicity goes way beyond just posting a flyer or putting an ad in the paper.

2. You should develop a publicity timeline; "set up" prewritten news releases and pictures (make it easy for the media to cover your event); create "staged" events (roll an Earthball down Main Street and call the paper); do "dog and pony" presentations at the local PTA; use home computer mailboxes, cable and PSAs; and get a proclamation from the mayor.

3. Keep a publicity file including all articles, videos, and good black-and-white glossy photographs.

4. Get to know your news people.

5. Stage miniplay sessions leading up to the event.

6. Your publicity strategy should peak just before the event. Use your timeline pre-event activities to educate and inspire folks to attend.

Presentation

1. This is it—The Event. Of course you have already made sure you have the keys, the field hasn't been watered the night before, and you have early access to the facility. What other details do you need to cover on the day of the event?

2. Where is everything going to be located? You've mapped it out beforehand so all of your people know what their day-of-event tasks are and where everything is supposed to go. We've found it helpful to have a day-of-event assigned task list and a logistics map and premade boxes of directions, supplies, and materials for all peripheral activities (e.g., the foot painting box, the giant bubbles box). This way you can easily store your boxes and re-place supplies for next year. You'll probably also want a larger map of where things are for the general public as they wander in. Where will you put the equipment depot, first-aid station, lost and found, refreshments, games booths, food? Why? And what are their interrelationships and how do they feed into each other, and help (and not hinder) each other? For example, can people easily

join a game after playing with the sidelines bubbles without having to walk 200 yards.

The Festival Day (the Event, the Play Itself)

Go for it. Other than logistics there are several operating principles that we believe will ensure a Big Fun, highly successful festival (or event). A festival, not unlike speeches, novels, a well-led game and life, has three main parts: a beginning, a middle, and an end. Actually there are a couple of beginnings and really three endings (but only *one* middle). Let's start at the beginning.

Beginning I

Before the participants arrive:

1. Safety is paramount, so have all of your leaders line up shoulder-to-shoulder and walk the field for any hazards (sprinkler heads, gopher holes, dog doo-doo). If any are identified they should be removed, covered, filled or mitigated in some other way (e.g., we put a traffic cone over hidden sprinkler heads). If indoors, have your leaders spread out and do the same, asking the question, what would be a potential hazard if someone was running out of control. Even a simple thing like a piece of loose-leaf paper on the floor can be deadly.

2. Next, establish a centralized equipment depot and an agreement with all the leaders that when they are finished with a piece of equipment, they return it to the central depot.

3. Make sure that your leaders have a finalized, organized, available, workable games list (this should be done at the training or prior to the event).

4. Psych your games leaders up with a Vince Lombardi/Robin Williams type speech, so just like at the Super Bowl, they will be ready to charge through the flaming entry ring and give their all to the festival and participants. A little huddle check here is often appropriate (enthusiasm is synergistic and contagious). And be sure to remind them that *they can have fun too* (if they are having fun everyone else will)!

5. Last but not least, remind them (in a 60-second group brainstorm) of *everything* that they have learned about play leadership and play events.

6. Keep the door open and get out of their way.

Beginning II

When real people start arriving (actually many of them have already arrived early because of your contagious enthusiasm and publicity):

1. The leaders should know that they have several different informal roles to play and that each is critical in these opening moments of the festival. Some will be "tour guides" ("and over here we have the Earthball games and over here we have the giant bubble pool"); some will be "greeters" ("Welcome. We're here to celebrate the day and each other. The games are simple—you can join and/or leave anytime you want or even suggest a game. We're playing for the fun of it. The games will change throughout the day. Big people can play too. Free admission—all you need is a smile"). Give the leaders a few key words that they can use; some leaders will be "matchmakers" ("Here's a Frisbee—you guys want to catch?" "Would you like your face painted?" "Would you hold the stilts for this kid?"); some will be "game initiators." This can be done by several leaders starting a game and inviting people to join or loudly announcing, "We're starting a game of Frisbee Football—everyone's welcome." All of these roles are important to help kick off the festival in a positive enthusiastic spirit. As the organizer you need to make sure people act on these roles right from the be-ginning (and not wander around aimlessly...do some nudging or side coaching if you need to).

2. People (participants) need enthusiastic, gentle "permission" to join a game and/or try something new. Access, choice, and invitation are important, but remember *no guilt trips* (people have the right not to play). Remember to see "shy" people's participation in stages. Maybe you've handed them a Frisbee and they are playing catch. Later you might come back to them and invite them to play Frisbee Golf or Frisbee Baseball!

3. Early game choices should include the following considerations:

a. Make sure a few of your early games are mixer, icebreaker, team-builder, defroster, and name-type games.

b. Integrate low-key trust games and physical (nonverbal) contact in a fun nonthreatening way early on (games like Touch Blue, 30-Second Handshakes, and People to People are examples of these).

c. Start with more familiar games (e.g., tag or parachute-type games) in the beginning, ones that people have a better handle on or are more familiar with. Save some of the eyes closed, weird sounds, heavy feely touchy, more intimidating games for later when people have started to feel more comfortable with themselves and others.

d. Teach your leaders good ways of rounding folks up. It's amazing if you walk through a crowd dragging a long rope or a parachute how many folks will grab on, especially if you say, "I need some help with this!" Also try a human train with the "engine" having a train whistle in his or her mouth. "All aboard!" It's amazing how many folks will attach themselves and before you know it you have enough players for your game. Or say you have only ten players but need more—send each of the ten out to recruit one or two more each. It works (most of the time).

e. Teach your leaders to work together in twos, threes, and fours to lead a game so one person is saying the words while another is setting up the boundaries and another is helping with the demonstration. Emphasize "giving away" what you would want as a leader who needed good team support (e.g., positive, responsive spirit, helpful actions).

f. Finally, in the early parts of the festival and really throughout the whole event, strive for a visual and actual variety of offerings—high-, low-, and medium-energy level, and different game types (e.g., theater-type games, quiet guessing, active sport-type games, games with equipment and without equipment). This allows people to see and sample these choices.

The Middle

Let's say a three-hour festival has been going on for about an hour or an hour and a half. What should we be doing? At this point it might be wise to review Chapter 4, *Keeping It Going*, for all of the principles of game change, facilitating Flow, and reenergizing activities. A few additional reminders:

1. Maintain the balance, choices, and flavors for people that were spoken about earlier so people continue to feel free to float, shop, sample, stay, and play.

2.   Be particularly aware of the energy level of both the players and the leaders. This may mean leaders "spelling" and/or supporting each other in a variety of other ways, lowering the energy level of the games, or maybe having a water balloon fight. One of the most powerful ways the leaders can support each other is by *using facilitative, supportive questioning strategies* as they are leading games together. So if someone who explains a game forgets a key rule, rather than you saying, "You idiot, you forgot to tell us what happens when we get tagged," see yourself as a "plant in the audience" who cleverly *asks* at that key time, "John, what happens when someone gets tagged?" The light bulb goes on in John's head! He tells the rule and it feels much better and more supportive. A Process Guardian (Angel)...

3.   Everyone must be ever-vigilant regarding safety throughout the entire festival—even more so on sunny hot days. Take water breaks, play games in the shade, or take appropriate short time-outs. Fatigue leads to injuries. Injuries are No Fun.

4.   Continue to be alert to regrouping and recentralizing equipment, which tends to "get legs," disperse and sometimes disappear during festivals. (Impacts on budgets are No Fun.)

Ending I

Festivals and events eventually wind down (yes; even fanatic players have to sleep, recover and get other needs met). So it is absolutely critical at the end of a festival to think of ways to bring positive closure to the event. People have been playing well and safely together for a few hours and we want to end that experience on an upbeat note so that folks will remember it that way and want to return for more. This is positive reinforcement for the playing community and an extension of empowerment. As with single games, we don't want to let it drop or cut it off abruptly:

1.   About 15 to 20 minutes before the event is scheduled to end, let the leaders know that on a centralizing signal (e.g., a moose horn) they are to end whatever game they are leading and bring all the people together for a big centralized closure game. It's usually good to also give them a five-minute warning so they can avoid ending their individual games abruptly. Then they communicate positive closure to their players.

2. An ending game should be a good metaphor for the "play community" that we've shared (see Chapter 5, *Ending It All Well*). So something that is circular or connective in nature is appropriate. Something where we all have to solve a simple task together and/ or have eye and hand contact with each other. Some of our favorite festival enders are the Lap Sit, Spirals, and the quick, but nonetheless effective, Huggle with a pat on the back option.

3. One thing that is very helpful is for "referees" to know in advance what their role is for the final game. In the Lap Sit for example it's very helpful for the leaders to do a minidemonstration Lap Sit in the middle of the large circle so the participants can see what they are going to do. Then the leaders can fan out and intersperse themselves at various parts of the circle to help out with munchkins or gaps in the circle. It's good also at this point to have a good attention getter so that everyone can focus in on the directions (see Chapter 3, *Getting It Going*).

4. After this final game ends, thank everyone for playing and have everyone give themselves a round of applause or a rousing cheer. And publicly thank the leaders, helpers, and sponsors (keep it short). Once again a reaffirmation of the energy and spirit of play!

5. At the end of this applause remind everyone that there is one last game: Eco-Ball. This reaffirms not only our connection to each other but also to the earth. And it is another one of our contributions back to the community. So have everyone line up shoulder-to-shoulder at one end of the field and walk the entire length of the field picking up any garbage, paper, broken water balloons, or other trash. By the time you reach the end of the field, the play space looks cleaner than when you got there. In indoor events people can fan out and do the same thing. People can also help round up any stray equipment and return it to the central equipment depot.

Ending II

As an event or festival ends we find that there are a few things that are important for the staff who lead the games and worked the peripheral activities:

1. First of all, everyone needs to help with pickup and cleanup. This will involve activities such as sorting the equipment and supplies into logical groupings, gathering any stray equipment, gathering

the trash, and returning tables and chairs. All of this help gets the job done quickly and acknowledges the last of the behind-the-scenes work.

2. We feel that it's also important to debrief the festival immediately with the leaders. See the Magic Pine Cone or Nerf ball technique in Chapter 5, *Ending It All Well*. This is a chance to complete the training cycle and to let leaders tell of their joys and horror stories, as well as what they learned about people in general, games and play, leadership, and festivals. Keep it brief and crisp and end with a leader hug and/or self-congratulating applause (for having survived and triumphed!).

3. Now everyone should go for pizza or have a major party to celebrate and positively reinforce his or her efforts (who knows, these alumni leaders may come back next year).

Endings III and Beginnings

Beginning preparations for next year:

1. Within two weeks of the festival there should be a comprehensive review and evaluation of the entire operation and of the event itself. This should involve all the committee members and any leaders and participants who want to attend.

2. At this evaluation meeting comprehensive records should be kept and the committee should systematically review all subcommittee (e.g., publicity, program, logistics) checklists and timelines and make recommendations regarding modifications and/or improvements.

3. Evaluation is really the ending and beginning of the new cycle. This meeting affirms and applauds all of the efforts of the group and gets ready for next year.

4. We think that this meeting should also be a celebration with food, drink, slides, and pictures so that the organizers end with positive reinforcement and enthusiasm for next year.

So at the end we should have that sense of "play community" reinforcement at three different levels: (a) at the end of festival for the participants, (b) after the festival for the leaders, and (c) during the evaluation for the organizers.

A Few Hot Events

This chapter ends with a brief description of a few hot play events that we've been connected with. The great thing is that new combinations and configurations are being developed and are only limited by your imagination. Some of these events happened yesterday and are ongoing (some happened a few yesterdays ago).

Dundercon—Magic Fest

Dundercon is a Dungeons and Dragons contest—pulling together hundreds of people who happen to like playing fantasy board and card games such as Dungeons and Dragons or Magic the Gathering into a grand space to share variations of this passion. People participating and finding their own group to play a game with and then drifting off from that group, joining another group and getting into a totally new game of D&D or Magic. The exciting thing about this is that it is just a model of pulling together any type of indoor game activity or game. It could be a Monopoly Convention or a miscellaneous board game event with Risk, Scrabble, Trivial Pursuit, The Settlers of Catan, Puerto Rico, and many other choices. *Games* magazine often reports on varieties of these types of events, including computer game festivals.

New Games Festival

A New Games Festival is a way to use active participatory games to bring people closer together. We use these games as a central part of the event to get people involved in acting together in small or large groups and at the same time build around that central core of new games, peripheral events such as bubble blowing, painting group murals, group weaving, jugglers, musicians, stilt walkers, board games, ad infinitum. These can support and provide a balance to the active involvement games in the middle area. New Games Festivals have been done with anywhere from several hundred people to 10,000 people and they have been done in countries all over the world.

Family Fun Festival

The Family Fun Festival is a spin-off of the New Games Festival with an emphasis on intergenerational play. It's a chance for families, no matter how they are defined, no matter how big they are, and friends of the family (family being very broadly defined as kin), to come together and to engage in all

kinds of activities that will promote family unity. All kinds of family activities can be built around the Family Fun Fest. In Pacifica, California, for example, we've created Family Fun Run with all kinds of different family categories, and Family Feud Contest where various family teams get together and engage in water bucket relay contests and balloon busting and things of that sort. Also a Young Artists' Contest was promoted in the schools: children drew pictures around the theme of "The Family That Plays Together." A wide variety of other activities were designed to reinforce play in the family. When people showed up at the Family Fun Festival, they also received a free booklet of very inexpensive and free family fun ideas for them to do at home and in their neighborhoods. So start to think about all the different things that can reinforce the concept of healthy family activity.

Spielfest

Spielfest is a German invention, taking off again from the New Games Festival concept, combining new games with traditional German games, play art and folk activities. At a *Spielfest* there would be new games and activities in a central area, and in the peripheral activities, there would be a number of game events based on traditional sports—everything from darts to Ping-Pong to badminton to soccer goal kicking to lawn bowling. People could go in and try some of these traditional activities or they could shift into the middle area of the field and participate in new games.

The Power of Play–Days of Play *(Tages de Spiel)*

The Power of Play–Days of Play *(Tages de Spiel)* is a three-day event held in the city of Munich put on by an incredible group called the *Pedagogische Aktion,* which means learning by doing. It combines workshops in everything from folk dancing to juggling to clowning to circus skills with actual participatory stations, events, and activities of the widest variety. Play ranges from new games activities to various stilts and cooperative equipment being laid out for the public to sample. Little minitheater reviews are ongoing and arts activities like giant papier-mâché mask making, are tied into the playlets; inflatable equipment and informal movement exploration spaces invite self-discovery. The whole event is spread out over the entire Olympic Stadium area, with more than 60 to 80 play stations run by *Pedagogische Aktion* and other visiting local, regional, and national play organizations.

Freedom Day

Freedom Day was an event that Bernie De Koven did for the city of Philadelphia during the U.S. bicentennial celebration. One of the unique things about this event was that it was virtually unfacilitated. That means that it didn't depend on creating numerous sets of creative and intriguing equipment. Rather, it was a concept of creating an event around the use of intriguing, attractive, captivating materials and then giving people the freedom to use those materials in any safe and playful way that they wished to. People wandered from one area of the park to another. They would come upon giant pick-up-sticks or giant playing cards or set of boffers, and this would stimulate them into developing their own ways of experimenting and playing.

Playfair Events

Last are Playfair Events. Originally Playfair was most well-known for doing college orientations and getting people to be able to interact at a very high level of energy. Their approach often involves a staged performance where there is a central person play leader (on a stage), who is orchestrating a variety of mixer, icebreaker, name-oriented kinds of activities. There are maybe a thousand people at these orientations, new freshman or new transfer students. The event is very highly orchestrated, very highly scripted, and very successful in terms of the level of interactions that it generates. Playfair has also promoted very tightly scripted events utilizing elements of games play, movement, and humorous interaction emphasizing the positive power of laughter and creativity in a corporate setting and the healing power of humor.

There are so many other incredible multimedia–multisensory Special Play Events around the world, including Interactive (a Munich event combining the best of high-tech and high-touch play activities), the Arizona Mud Olympics (imagine what a Mud parcourse would look like), Glendale, California's Christmas in July (with imported snow), and myriad celebrations held on sidewalks, in children's museums, in pools, and in warehouses. The bottom line in looking at all of these events is to be able to draw from them the elements and flavors that you need for your own events. Remember that an event is nothing more than a big game that multiplies the possibilities for positive playful interaction. If you apply the principles mentioned in this chapter with the long-term necessary logistics and committee work, you're sure to have a highly successful play event.

Chapter 8

Advanced Leadership Skills

Only when he no longer knows what he is doing does the painter do good things.

—Edgar Degas

Unless you have been thoroughly drenched in perspiration you cannot expect to see a palace of pearls on a blade of grass.

—*Blue Cliff Record*

What we'll be talking about in this chapter is the Playmeister, the Playerama Man, the Wonder-Game Woman, the Magister Ludi (Master Player) Lady, the Johnny or Joanie Playmaker who has taken his or her leadership to another level of understanding and practice. Beyond the basics. Beyond the fundamentals. A person who has led a good number of games with a variety of groups in many different settings. At least a *level four play leader*. Remember in the Preface of this book we identified four levels of the learning-leading process:

1. *Unconscious Incompetence*. You are not any good at being a leader, but you don't know it (so it doesn't matter).

2. *Conscious Incompetence*. You realize you are not very good. You want to get good, but you know it's going to take a lot of work and play.

3. *Conscious Competence*. With conscious thought, planning, effort, and dedication, you do a very competent job as a play leader.

4. *Unconscious Competence*. As a play leader, you have that sixth sense. You still have to do a bit of planning, but you just seem to know how to do the right thing at the right time. That certain game. That certain adjustment. Those certain words that evoke a smile and inspire new levels of playfulness, togetherness, and happiness in a group. Your integration of group dynamics, knowledge, and advanced leadership skills, and your deeply ingrained play spirit enable you to playfully respond to the world whether in informal situations or professional contexts. The Playmeister, traveling the world, planting and nurturing seeds of play wherever you go! Smiles, tickles, giggles, guffaws, hos, ho hos, ho ho hos, snickers, joy.

This chapter is about making the transition from level 3 to level 4 (and beyond). Besides continuous practice, there are at least five areas that an advanced leader must understand:

1. *Flow Theory and Implications*. Being able to understand the elegance of Flow and facilitate its power.

2. *Empowerment*. To "let go," transfer, and share the power to Flow, create, and change with the group.

3. *The Art of Play Leadership*. Moving beyond the craft and technical aspects of leadership to shape and enhance the play experience and all of its potential richness so that each game is vivid and three dimensional and, thus, allows the players to fully express their joyful humanity.

4. *Situational Leadership*. How you flexibly utilize different styles, approaches, modifications, and challenges for different groups in different settings.

5. *Positive, Assertive Discipline*. Hints, techniques, approaches, and strategies for maintaining a motivating and focused environment in an imperfect world.

A concentrated understanding and dedicated practice of each of these five areas will help bring you up to another exciting level of personal and professional growth.

Flow

Simply put, Flow is a state of high enjoyment. It is when people are having Big Fun and/or high levels of satisfaction in a work or play situation. Flow was identified as a concept by the eminent social psychologist Dr. Mihaly Csikszentmihalyi (from now on referred to as Dr. C), who has studied this phenomena for over 25 years. He was interested in the qualities that accompanied high states of involvement, enjoyment, and arousal during work or play activities, and his subjects have included thousands of blue- and white-collar workers, athletes, dancers, rock climbers, and chess players—people from almost every walk of life and level of ability. His findings have tremendous implications for personal quality of life issues as well as professional practice. Perhaps the best summary of his work is to be found in his book *Flow: The Psychology of Optimal Experience—Steps Toward Enhancing the Quality of Life*. You are encouraged to fully explore this book and other Flow references listed in Chapter 12, *Resources, Connections, and Beyond*. For our purposes however, we would like to focus on the aspects of Flow theory that have direct application to advanced professional leadership skills whether they be applied in a single game or an entire play festival. We firmly believe that in addition to the development of the play community, the facilitation of flow is the main goal of play leadership.

The Fun Zone

Flow occurs somewhere between boredom and anxiety and is influenced by the individual player's *perception* of his or her ability and the challenge at hand.

If the person's (or group's) ability clearly exceeds the challenge, there will be boredom. Likewise, if the challenge exceeds the person's (or group's) ability, there will be anxiety. Think about the difference between playing tick-tack-toe with your friend (boredom) or hang gliding off a cliff without lessons (anxiety). To keep your activity in the Flow zone, the trick for you as a game leader or player, will be to find (and fine tune) that balance between boredom and anxiety. Luckily, we all know it when we're there. Think about when you are playing a good game of racquetball with someone with whom you are evenly matched. The outcome is uncertain. The lead goes back and forth. You're in the moment...focused in...you've lost track of time and you're having fun. You're Flowing. These are the best games. Or take a tag game as an example. The best ones are when there is an equally unpredictable possibility that you'll get caught or you'll get away. It's doable but you're just not sure how it's going to come out. As a leader you can fine-tune the game so it will have this elegance. It's not unlike a master violinist. If the strings on his or her instrument are too tight, they screech; if they are too loose, they moan; if they are tuned just right, they make beautiful music.

Dr. C found that although games, play, and adventure activities were different than Flow, their flexibility and ability to manipulate their elements (e.g., rules, boundaries, strategies) made them have great potential for evoking Flow states. And, one of the great things about "new games" activities is that they often have very simple rules (that can be changed) and yet many strategic possibilities.

In addition to this need for fine tuning the game, Dr. C's findings on Flow states suggest several implications for lifestyle enhancement and advanced play facilitation. The lifestyle implications are derived directly from the main qualities of Flow reported by the hundreds of subjects studied by Dr. C. These implications suggest that you:

1. Have a range of challenges or complexities that you can fine tune.

2. Focus your attention; narrow your stimulus field.

3. Integrate novelty, dissonance, and/or risk into your existence (e.g., surprises, new activities, new places—break set for rearousal).

4. Minimize time consciousness in present (escape clocks, be in the moment).

5. Minimize outcome focus and future extrinsic rewards (be "process aware").

6. Relax and be aware of your body and sense (stress reducing, focusing, and sensory awareness activities).

7. Obtain and/or give immediate positive feedback (support systems).

These implications are equally valid for leadership and these are the ones we will focus on. Before beginning this list it's important to remind ourselves that in addition to helping others to achieve Flow, we need to set up situations for ourselves as leaders so we can achieve it, so we have the proper level of challenge, so after doing the same game over and over we change it appropriately so we too are "rearoused."

Some Practical Implications of Flow Theory

Get and focus attention by using good attention getters. People in flow states report conditions of a narrowed stimulus field. If people are "all over the map" (e.g., looking in six different directions with a lot of cross talk, or are easily distracted from the game or each other by blaring music next to the playing field), then it's much more difficult to achieve a Flow State. So whether it's in a single game or festival, use the attention-getting techniques described in Chapter 3, *Getting It Going*. They will help people zone in.

Fine tune the game challenge for initial Flow or for rearousal. We've alluded to this earlier (see Chapter 4, *Keeping It Going*, and Chapter 6, *On Games*). So, if necessary, modify the game for bigger fun, for safety, and for difference. Shrink the boundaries, add more "its," change the rules, add more equipment, and change the way people move. For example, what if we were playing a game of Hug Tag and we were running around and the only time that we were safe was when we were hugging somebody in this game. We've one person who is "it" and he or she is identified as "it" because he or she has a Frisbee and he or she chases people trying to hand that Frisbee to someone who is not hugging someone. If we have 60 people out there and one tagger is running around, there are a whole lot of people who are standing not doing too much. So we might change it and make two people with Frisbees in their hand both "it." So now we have a little more action going on in this game. The challenge is a little harder for the people who are trying to get away, and a little easier for those people who are trying to tag folks.

If that is not enough, then add a third "it," a fourth "it," until the game is "tuned." From there we might find out that people seem to be hugging forever. They are just getting into it because it's too much fun (a little bit of a different game in and of itself), but this is also breaking down the possibility of some real running interaction and challenging opportunity of trying to get away from the taggers. So we might come up with a hugging rule, where people can only hug for five seconds, for example, or they can only hug for the time that they can in fact take a deep breath and hum together (breathe in, "wwhhhoooooii, hummmmmmmmmmmmmm"). OK, when we run out of air, then we must separate and run. And so what we've done is to look at the interactions of the activity and perhaps do whatever it takes to fine-tune the challenge of the game activity. That helps keep us out of the boredom area and out of the anxiety area.

Use novelty and dissonance to "break set" and to get people's juices going again. You might recall (from Chapter 5, *Ending It All Well*) that each game or event has an arousal plateau (or a series of plateaus). You can use novelty or difference or change at this point to help get people back in the Flow Zone. This might be especially true if you're meeting a group over a series of weeks or if they have played certain games before. Your novelty might be wearing a funny hat, wearing two different shoes, calling a game of Hug Tag, "Bug Tag," and creating a whole new fantasy about sticky buzzing hives of nuclear mutated arachnoids. It might be standing in a different place or starting your presentation with a moose horn. Whatever it is, by using novelty and dissonance, by breaking set, by changing routine, you increase the probability of more folks getting (back) into the Flow Zone.

Minimize time consciousness—Help people to play in the present moment. One of the most reported qualities of Flow, by people in the experience, was a lack or loss of time consciousness. Time was altered (either sped up or slowed down). When they were Flowing, people weren't checking their watches. They were having a good time and were in the moment. This immersion in the experience and escape from the jaws of the time machine is vital for health in our "hurry sickness" society. So what can you do as game-play leaders to help facilitate this experience for people? As much as possible with your facility and institutional constraints, create flexible or open-ended time schedules and foster client-responsive flexible leadership. Cover up the clocks on the wall in the gym. Ask people to take their watches off. Run a three-hour festival where the games are constantly changing in response to the players' needs as opposed to an artificially preestablished schedule (see Chapter 7, *Events or the Big Game*).

It truly breaks the flow when you're having a great time playing jacks and someone comes along, blows a whistle in your ear and says, "It's 1:30— time for Hula-Hoops and don't forget at 2:00 p.m. it's sack races!" Maybe you just hadn't peaked yet with jacks! Think about it. When we're having a great time at a party or in a game, we aren't watching our watches. That is why we were always late when we were kids coming home from play. We got lost in the Flow.

Minimize the external rewards and outcomes of the activity. Help the players be *process*-oriented because Flow is a process concept. The fun is in the doing. Sure its nice to "win" in the traditional sense of the word but that is the icing on the cake. Quit flashing a trophy in front of us and reminding us about the score. If we're having fun, learning, growing, then we're all "winners" regardless of the outcome of a particular contest. Quit focusing on the external when Flow is mostly about internal consciousness. "Yeah, but if I play this game, what do I get for it?" A good time and Big Fun! Very tough to do in a consumer society where the trophies are sometimes bigger than the kids.

Help people to Flow more by helping them to relax and to tune into their bodies and senses. You just can't Flow if you're negatively stressed out or generally oblivious. Play at its best makes the world vividly technicolored and three-dimensional. You might have noticed that several of the games in the original *New Games* books and the current *Project Adventure* books (see Chapter 12, *Resources, Connections, and Beyond*) have elements of touch, expressiveness, or eyes closed qualities. It's no accident. In fact a few (People Pass, Trust Walks, and Cradle) were borrowed from the human potential movement of the late '60s, and a few others from classic theater games sources like Viola Spolin's *Improvisation for the Theater*. There is something about the nonverbal connection and/or the sensory deprivation or expression (e.g., eyes closed or mirroring someone) that does get us more "in touch." These activities also help us operate more from an integrative right brain or whole person perspective, and get up appropriately "out of our heads" (our Western culture linear cognitive analytic selves) into a more holistic playful place. So in addition to all we've said about the creation of psychological safety zones, try some relaxation, sensory awareness, or "safe touch" games to increase the potential for Flow. People will tune in more to the moment and themselves (aka, *be here now*).

When in Flow situations, provide accessible immediate feedback. If people have played well, played safely, played Flowingly, positively reinforce it using any of the techniques described in Chapter 5, *Ending It All Well* (e.g., applause, pats on the back). This helps folks recognize Flow and increases the desire not only to repeat it, but also to surround themselves with a Flow social support system of fellow players. Good job!

A Few More Wolf Tickets

For those of you who haven't figured it out, *wolf* is *flow* spelled backwards. "Who's afraid of the Big Bad Flow? Tra la la la la." The seven major principles just listed definitely work to facilitate more Flow for folks. But we've found out a few other things along the way that seem to help, too, in facilitating play–gamc Flow and we would like to briefly list these:

- Use similar game "types" in sequence to keep the energy going with very slight shifts in rules (e.g., go from Elbow Tag to Loose Caboose to Catch the Dragon's Tail). In each tag game you're trying to "attach yourself" as part of the action.

- Use similar game formations in sequence. Do a whole series of circle games (e.g., go from Zoom to Birthday Lineup to People to People).

- Pay attention to the energy level of games. Sequence them so each successive game has a higher energy level than the last *or* as folks are getting tired the activities move in the opposite energy direction, winding down. Or better yet, plan flexibly and ask them which energy direction they want to go toward. Another useful segue metaphor is to think of an outstanding play leader as an excellent deejay who gets people up and out on the floor dancing, going smoothly and seamlessly from one song to the next, paying attention to his or her audience and using the right selection from his or her musical repertoire. And all of a sudden people have been out on the floor for 45 minutes—Flowing.

- Use themes to help create Flow. This is obvious around holidays but need not be confined to them. Scary or "death" games on Halloween are good examples. But you might just as easily program a series of balloon games (Balloon Volleyball, Balloon Stomp, Fire in the Hole, Water Balloon Whompies), or games using just old newspapers (Newspaper Relay, Find It in the Papers, Mummy Wrap).

- Use music to create Flow. We've had a lot of fun making tapes that facilitate fun ways to move, to warm up, to energize to play certain games, and to warm down and relax. Some of these tunes also provide some not so subliminal messages (e.g., The Walk of Life; Fun, Fun, Fun; Too Much Fun; Three Little Birds [Don't Worry About a Thing]; One Heart, One Love) that help set a mood for Fun and Flow.

- What other ways can you think of? (Tra la la la la...)

More on Flow, Energy, and Sequencing

- The advanced leader needs to be sensitive to sequencing and energy in relation to Flow. Remember, the goal is to build increased intimacy and community (see also Chapter 3, *Getting It Going*, and Chapter 4, *Keeping It Going*, for hints on sequencing).

- That sense of community might include higher levels of physicality, expressiveness, flexibility, and communication in the games that we play.

- Reading your group needs and planning flexibly is vital. Am I starting too early in my play sequences with activities that are too silly or too touchy-feely or too "different," or too physical (before the group is ready)? Step back in the midst of your planned sequence and ask, "What have the group members revealed to me so far about themselves? Are they loose? Do they have a good sense of humor? Are they plunging in? Where do we go from here? Do we jack up the energy? Do we need to go a little more slowly and build trust?"

- It's always important to start from where people are (regardless of where you think they should be or where you want to take them). For example, does a corporate group need an initial task-oriented game or a mixer icebreaker that pays attention to the corporate culture? Does a group of "sit down" childcare directors need a simple energizing tag game to start off with (not only because their energy is low but because most everyone is familiar with the concept of tag).

- Remember, if we do all of the above, we're helping people get into the Fun Zone (aka, Flow Channel). Once they are there we can build on it.

Flow and "It" Power

You may recall that in Chapter 6, *On Games*, we talked about game change and the importance of modifying activities to facilitate Flow, for safety reasons, for novelty and for rearousal. An understanding of "It" Power is vital for the advanced leader.

"It" Power Defined

Simply put, "It" Power is the power of the "It" (whether it be a guesser or a tagger) to have a relatively moderate probability of success in a game that nevertheless has an unpredictable outcome for all the participants. That means that I should be able to catch you but you should have an "equal" chance of getting away.

"It" Power is about the challenge of a game and how it can be fine tuned to facilitate Flow for all the players. So if Bill is not catching you in a tag game (and has little hope of doing it), Bill is not having any fun (Bill is anxious), but the reality is that you aren't having any fun either (you are bored). In this case the "It" Power is too low and it isn't doing much for Bill's self-esteem (or the general fun). So the trick is how we can fine tune the "It" Power and create more of a *win–win,* self-esteem building atmosphere.

Some Ways To Moderate the "It" Power

- In tag, add more "its" or helpers.

- Think of the golf or bowling concept of "handicapping" (e.g., only tag with one arm, change the way folks move, shrink the boundaries, add more balls to create Ball Tag).

- In guessing games, use a team of guessers (you can always make it harder), teach creative hint giving, change the position of the guessers, ask the group members to make their movements more obvious or to make changes at a preset time (e.g., every 15 seconds).

- Starting signals—Should the runners begin running when the leader says, "1-2-3 Octopus..." or at random or on delayed starts (much lower "It" Power than with a set signal) or should the leader call each individual by name to run (much higher "It" Power)?

- Position of the "It" and/or the players—Was she somewhere in the middle of the field when she gave her starting signal or right next to the line of people (higher power), facing the runners or with her back turned (lower power)? Do the runners race all at once from one safety zone to another or from two, three, or four directions?

- Use a cumulative versus a replacement "it"—that is as you get tagged you become part of Bill's tagging team (instead of replacing Bill) and the collective "It" Power grows.

You get the idea. Change the games to fit the people and keep it in the Fun Flow Zone. As people become more comfortable and skilled you can always moderate the challenge level. And don't forget to ask them for their suggestions.

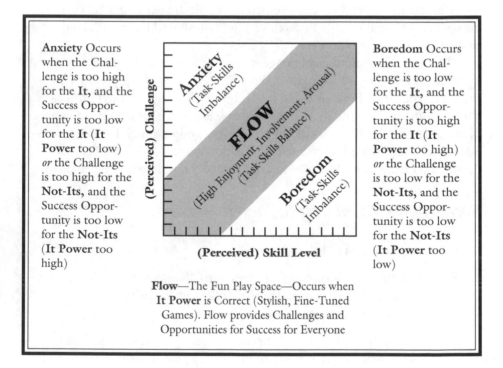

Anxiety Occurs when the Challenge is too high for the **It,** and the Success Opportunity is too low for the **It** (**It Power** too low) *or* the Challenge is too high for the **Not-Its,** and the Success Opportunity is too low for the **Not-Its** (**It Power** too high)

Boredom Occurs when the Challenge is too low for the **It,** and the Success Opportunity is too high for the **It** (**It Power** too high) *or* the Challenge is too low for the **Not-Its,** and the Success Opportunity is too low for the **Not-Its** (**It Power** too low)

Flow—The Fun Play Space—Occurs when **It Power** is Correct (Stylish, Fine-Tuned Games). Flow provides Challenges and Opportunities for Success for Everyone

In Summary

As an advanced leader, if you (a) can learn to plan for and to facilitate the proper level of "It" Power to create high-Flow situations, and (b) can recognize non-Flow (flux) in the play session and "fix it" (fine-tune the experience), you are in a position of highly positive control of the situation.

It's at this level that it really gets exciting, because you as a leader are in a position to "let go" to be more vulnerable to experiment and to take more risks (knowing that you can always realign things). You can truly be "in the moment," pay attention to the spontaneous play of the group, and experience the wonder, the natural Flow and freedom that playfulness at its best truly is.

Psychological Safety Zones

Throughout this book we've talked a lot about how important psychological safety is for keeping the activity in the Fun Zone for the players. In addition to our positive ways of picking teams, our game change and "It" Power suggestions, here are a few other specific examples of how to create psychological safety:

- In Birthday Lineup (where everyone lines up in a circular formation [without talking] according to the day and month they are born), use a magic marker in the center of the circle that you all agree to point at in case someone is out of sequence (and say, "Oh, look, a magic marker"). This allows the players to "sneak" into correct position without feeling inadequate (because we've created this funny ritual).

- In People to People and The Wind Blows (where there is one person "leftover" in the middle) as everyone scurries to find a chair or partner, say that "it's an honor and privilege to lead us in the next round" (turning a negative into a positive). Also teach players strategies to reduce "central person anxiety" (they can tell every one "who has clothes on" to run and get a new chair and that will increase their chances of getting a chair and not being stuck out there).

- In Knots allow the "surgery" technique where the group members, if they wish, can unclasp and reclasp any one set of hands to untangle the knot.

- Use "permission words" (e.g., "give it your best shot" or "in life and games you don't have to be perfect").

- Use pledges (have the group members raise their right hands and repeat "I don't have to be perfect" or "I am a safety monitor" or "I am a person of high integrity").

- Use group support and positive reinforcement techniques (e.g., applause for good effort, welcoming the next leader into the circle).

- Use games like Cooperative Musical Chairs (or Hoops or Ruglets) to change the end result by keeping everyone *in* the game.

- Use parallel or spillover games like Parallel Simon Says, where people eliminated from one game get to join another game.

- Use time limits to keep things moving and give people a lot of turns (e.g., in Frisbee Baseball we play five outs or five minutes for each half inning, whichever comes first [this also usually avoids 73 to 4 scores]).

- Play shorter games for fewer points with rematches (e.g., in Balloon Volleyball we play three-point games so I know I'll live to have another shot at it even if I lose).

- Teach strategies for success (e.g., in Frisbee Baseball we teach kids to throw the disk in weird ways so it is less catchable).

- Or create other roles for those who are "eliminated" (e.g., "hecklers" in Zen Clap, fielders when folks make an out in Everybody Bats Baseball).

In what other ways can we create *emotional safety* in play and still keep it fun and challenging?

Empowerment

Lao Tzu said many thousands of years ago that as a leader you grow stronger as you give away and share power. As an advanced leader you are not an autocratic authority. Rather you let others take charge and make suggestions, but you are still there to support them and to facilitate the experience. Your goal is to guide them to discover and to develop their individual and collective responsibility for their own playfulness—the highest form of responsibility.

An empowered game–play experience can be an important metaphor for participation in the world, for developing problem solving and initiative in the world, and for people to believe that they can affect their world positively. This is vital today when so many folks are alienated from their institutions and believe that there is no hope and nothing they can do to change the world. Empowering games leadership contributes to democratic interactive citizenship, because people are being asked to be participators, producers, and creators versus blindly accepting authority and being mesmerized by passive consumer entertainment media. The research is clear: believing that you can change and that you can affect the world is a vital component of life success. There are a lot of ways to *empower* a group. We've included a few (see pp. 128–129). Can you think of any others?

Zen and the Art of Play Leadership

At some stage of mastery, the leader moves from being very good at the "craft" or science of leadership (all of the techniques) and starts to move into the realm of spontaneity, creativity freedom, and being in the moment that marks the difference between craft and art. It's said that before Picasso found his own way of painting, he was trained and practiced in classical styles and techniques. His early work shows this. As a play leader, it's as if you are painting a picture with great skill and dexterity, but also continue to add spirit, style, and spontaneity all your own.

So we have these different techniques. As we move to this level of mastery, we see our palate having more colors on it and we are open to more ways to use them. These colors are our opportunity to create themes, rituals, and fantasies around a game, and to paint a rich portrait of experience within the game itself (or within a series of games). We can do this by telling little stories; by creating wonderful fantasies, funny characters, and voices; and by encouraging the participatory interaction of humor and camaraderie between the players and leaders that enhances the colors of our collective experience.

Let's take a game like Star Wars Dodge Ball and describe the wonderful game in a rich colorful way:

> There are two forces in the universe, the dark side and the light side. And these forces have contended with each other in a final encounter. On the one side we have Darth Vader, and on the other side we have Luke Skywalker. (At this point, have the group play [by using "mouth sounds"] the theme from *Star Wars* softly in the background ["da da da, da da da da, da da da da da, da da da da"].) Now each of these sides are separated from the other by a force field. (Demonstrate the power of the force field ["Bzz, zzz, Bzzz"].) They can't physically touch each other, but what they can do is try to immobilize each other through the power of their Death Stars (which look amazingly like Nerf balls). Now, each side has its Death Stars and throws them through the force field to try to hit the storm trooper on the other side. If a storm trooper is hit by a Death Star, that storm trooper is "stunned senseless" and has to kneel down on the ground assuming a position of being "stunned senseless." (What an appropriate time to dramatically demonstrate being stunned senseless.) This is a pretty drastic situation that nobody would want to be in, but fortunately, there is the possibility of salvation. That is, if the one designated Jedi Knight in each team holding his or her light saber (which looks amazingly like a boffer), touches the storm trooper, who is stunned senseless, and can take him or her back to touch the

22 Ways to Empower a Group

1. Let the group chose what game to play.

2. Have someone in the group demonstrate the activity you are going to do.

3. Have the people in the group lay out the boundary lines for the game.

4. Have people help you carry all the equipment out to the field.

5. Have a game in which everybody takes a high-visibility role at some point in the game, such as Instant Replay (a "name" mimic game).

6. Play a game that requires a rotation of captains or primary leaders, where everyone in the group gets a chance to be captain, or over the course of time, gets to be a leader.

7. Use some games that break down into small teams (e.g., twos, threes, or fours) that have to make decisions and come up with strategies or rules to share with the rest of the group. In a small group like this, players are pushed to participate at a very high level, rather than just hiding out behind a loud, natural, or experienced leader.

8. Set up a day where everyone brings a game that is his or her favorite game to share so that we can all play.

9. Have some games where people take turns doing things that are rather risky and scary, such as doing a Trust Fall, or stepping in front of the group and singing their favorite song. Create an atmosphere of support and positive rein-forcement.

10. When a question comes up about a rule change, call a "team meeting" and have everybody discuss it and vote on how that rule is going to be played for the remainder of the game.

11. Put a piece of equipment in every person's hand or place a playing card in everyone's hand and say, "Hold this until the next set of instructions." For example, what if you walked into a room and put a Nerf ball into every person's hand? What would they think might happen next?

12. Have everyone simultaneously throw that Nerf ball at the leader who just walked into the room.

22 Ways to Empower a Group (continued)

13. Get into the practice of saying, "I don't know. What do you think? What would you like to do? How should we fix, play, or solve that?"

14. Have everyone carry the leader down to the field to play the game (much easier than the reverse).

15. Ask everyone invited to a potluck meal to bring really good food, fun food, or food to play with. Potlucks are gustatory empowerment rituals.

16. Have people bring a favorite toy or plaything to an event to share (or wear a favorite playful hat, button, or T-shirt).

17. Have everyone walk the field prior to leading any games activity to make sure that it's safe. This encourages everyone to assume responsibility for each other's safety.

18. Before and after an event, have the whole group walk the entire field or play space to make sure that there's no trash or litter left around. This empowers them to positively control and care for their play environment.

19. Teach people to ask for standing ovations. At any time they can stand up in front of the group and say, "You know, I deserve a standing ovation, and I'd really like one right now" (create a super fun ritual where everyone honors their request).

20. Laugh at other people's jokes while you're playing in the games and validate other people for contributing their humor and "clever" remarks to the general level of camaraderie and funniness of a play event. This encourages and empowers people to contribute more of this foolishness.

21. Empower your partner to continue to push ahead.

22. Empower your partner to quit when you know that you're both worn out and can't come up with any other bright ideas for ways to empower other people.

starbase (which looks amazingly like a Frisbee) deep within their territory, the force is once again within them and they are able to go back into battle. If the Jedi Knight should get stunned senseless, while off the starbase, that entire side of the universe is lost and the battle is over.

Or we could describe the same game this way:

Now we have this game where we have two teams of players who have a dividing line in the middle. We take balls and we throw them at each other, and you can't cross the line. If you get a ball thrown at you and it hits you, you can't move, and you have to crouch down. There is also a base and a guy who has a long stick who can come and get you back to the base and then you can go back and you can play again.

Which game description has been painted with a richer palate? Which one is going to give the players the greatest opportunity to dig into their playfulness, fantasy, creativity, sense of humor, and rituals, and create that kind of freedom space to explore high levels of play? The answer is clear (begin *Star Wars* theme).

In any game or play situation, you have the opportunity to take the explanation of leadership and maintenance of that game, and turn it into art. One way you'll know that it is art is when you're playing on the "edge." You feel excited, challenged and thrilled about your participation in the game as both a leader and a player. And so do the folks around you!

The challenge is, as you continue in your career as a play leader, and have led some games, maybe hundreds of times, how do you continue to improve your craft and to perfect the art of your leadership? How do you rejuvenate and recreate yourself so that presentation becomes an inspiration for the people playing, and an excitement for them to live and play a little more brightly and enthusiastically?

A recent example makes this clear. We had been playing Quick Line Up for the 4,000th time. It's a great high-energy "can't miss" game, where a line of players has to quickly regroup, line up, clasp hands, throw their arms up and shout "quick line up." Three other teams are trying to do the same thing. All lines start in a shoulder-to-shoulder formation with each team occupying one side of a square formation. A great game but it was starting to get a little flat after 3,999 times. One day John said, "One team should be the North team, one South, one East, and one West." The teams should huddle and come up with a quickly shared ritual chant that symbolizes their "region" (e.g., "West, West is the best;" "the South shall rise again"). So now when they realigned, they would shout their regional chant. Well, it changed and revitalized the whole game and opened up all kinds of new possibilities, with new rituals—all expressive, creative and empowering elements. It was an artistic moment.

Situational Leadership

Simply put, situational leadership is flexibility. What is your ability to plan and/or adapt appropriately for change or difference? How will you, as an advanced leader, modify your style, approach, language, demeanor, dress, and activity equipment selection for the (endless) variety of play leadership circumstances you'll encounter and, of course, for any of the elements of those circumstances (i.e., the players, the situation, the settings, the games).

The best of situational leadership consciousness comes from a ton of practice (including making a lot of mistakes); drawing on your full range of skills, techniques, and artistry; and developing an intuition as to what is appropriate. It's a lifelong learning process. As an advanced leader, take this opportunity to review your basic planning principles found in Chapter 3, *Getting It Going*, but then continue to develop your sensitivities to another level. Here are a few examples:

The Players

- What are their characteristics (e.g., physical, emotional, cultural)?

- What does their culture say about being male or female? about touching? about being publicly silly? about "winning"?

- What is appropriate language for the group (e.g., street jive, business technical, problem-solving language, or age-appropriate children's language)?

- What is the level of peer consciousness and influence? of risk taking ability? of expressiveness? of intimacy?

- What is their sense of humor?

- What is their need for direction and control versus freedom and exploration?

- How long have they been together? Under what circumstances? What else is there about the group dynamic? How tight are they?

- What is their level of caring and connectedness?

- What is their level of individual and collective safety consciousness?

After making a broad-based assessment of the players, how do you then choose activities, sequences, and a style that is appropriate? It might just be the tone or language you use. Obviously if you are playing with a group of high-school football players, the way you talk to them, the games you choose to play, the type of jokes you make, the way you get them together, and the ways you build a rapport with them are going to be radically different from the way you are going to build a rapport with a group of senior citizens in a convalescent home or a bunch of kindergartners. So have a plan. You can always change if you have a plan, but if you don't have one, it is hard to recoup and find another way to do it.

The Setting

The second circumstance that leaders encounter and have to respond to is different types of settings. The setting could be as diverse as playing out in a wide open grassy space; playing indoors in a closet; playing underwater in a swimming pool; playing in 105° heat with very little shade; playing in a huge ballroom with hundreds of round tables and eight people sitting at each table; playing in a very bare, dust covered field with half an inch of dirt and dust and no grass; or playing in the dark. As an advanced leader who has played in each of these settings you'll have sharpened your perceptions about what is appropriate for each of these in terms of style, content, and techniques. It's clear that each setting provides its own unique *opportunities* and *restrictions*.

Two of the main factors to focus on here are (1) safety and (2) *the fun potential* of the setting. Can you imagine and visualize what the fun potential might be for these settings and what some of the safety issues might be? (Be sure to review safety in both Chapter 2, *The Fundamentals of Play Leadership*, and Chapter 7, *Events or the Big Game*.) Something as simple as modifying your tone of voice could have a profound influence on the success of the play event. Given the fun and safety factors within a setting, maybe you need a more "serious" tone, or a problem-solving tone or, perhaps, a tone deliberately encouraging chaos! Style, content, techniques, tone and many other factors will vary greatly given the opportunities and restrictions of the setting. How can you open up your players to the potentials for innovation and fun and at the same time make them aware of potential hazards?

The Situation

Let's ask a simple question in regard to the play situation. Would your leadership style and your tone be different if you were leading activities at a birthday party, as opposed to a wake? The answer is yes (depending, of course, on who died and who's birthday it was). We introduced the concept of "the situation" earlier in Chapter 3, *Getting It Going*. Here we want to elaborate, give you a few examples and some problem-solving questions.

The situation might be anything from the Christmas holidays to a com_____, retreat, where the people have been sitting and listening to a long and boring lecture by a financial analyst for the two and a half hours and now it is your turn to lead games with them. Or maybe you go to work with kids during the monsoon season and they have been locked up in a classroom for two and a half months watching the rain outside. The situation is any set of circumstances that create a context for the players before, during, and even after the time you'll be playing with them. You must be prepared to contend with this context. What will be your activity or game choice and organizing methods? How will you vary your tone, your style in your techniques, and your language—in other words, all of what goes into your leadership to respond to each situation? How will you make it work (play)?

Some Examples

Let's look at a couple of examples of how leadership might change as the context of players, setting, and situation change.

Let's take the game of Knots. This is a game where a circular group of six to ten folks clasp hands creating a tangle and then proceed to untangle the knot without letting go of hands and by stepping over and under arms and legs until they arrive at a hand holding circle. Let's say we're playing with a group of college kids (the players) in a gymnasium (the setting) for an orientation program (the situation). This tells us that the kids probably don't know each other very well, and they probably want to get to know each other, yet they are shy and need encouragement. Given this, we might introduce the game of Knots fairly simply without much ado and structure to get everybody to tangle. We might ask them to get in a group of six with nobody that they know. (A group of six will create an easier first solution). We might ask the group members to introduce themselves, give them a practice round or two, and then challenge them to untangle as quickly as they can and shout, "We did it," when finished. To add even more energy to the game we might create a challenge between all the groups of six to see who can get untangled first. Our goal here is mostly just to promote fun ice-breaking interaction, so we don't want to have too much structure, or too many directions. Just let them play with it to see what they come up with. Keep it simple. If they start to bog down or get stuck we might introduce the concept of "knot aide" or "surgery" or "magic" ways to change hands around to make it easier to get out of the knot. If it's too easy, we might make the group bigger or change the challenge in some other way (make it nonverbal or have their eyes closed). But we'll let that wait until it's needed rather than introduce it in the beginning so that they can get deeply involved in the task.

Suppose we had the same game with a group of business folks in a team-building seminar who are dressed in restrictive business clothing. Perhaps with this group, touching or close physical interaction might also be an issue so we might deal with that by using three-foot lengths of rope that people can hold on to that connects them up to the other people in their circle. (This provides a bit more physical distance and ease of movement). Also, to make the game intriguing and appropriate to the players, we might frame our presentation of the game as follows:

> This is a problem-solving challenge. You are the problem-solving committee of a major corporation and you have the task of trying to figure out the most difficult, knottiest problem, that your corporation has ever encountered. It's up to you to find the best solution to this knotty problem, and it's important to pay attention to the communication, planning and decision-making process as you solve it.

This gives the group a certain familiar framework and orientation, and it also legitimizes participating in a physical activity as a real business learning exercise. With this group we might also vary the challenge level, add competition or time limit constraints, and we would definitely debrief re: communication, decision-making, and problem-solving skills.

Playing Knots with a group of people in wheelchairs and some folks who are not in wheelchairs, who haven't met each other, you might also use the "rope extension method" (this allows the ropes to be lowered and the chairs to roll over them), but your tone and approach might be very, very different. It might be softer and you might ask, "How can we figure all this out together?" Your emphasis might be more on making it happen for the entire group versus the "correctness of solution." Then again, depending on the maturity, initial success, and perceived ability of the group, you might want to jack up the challenge and change your tone. Suppose you had college business students in wheelchairs?

Finally, if you're leading Knots with fourth graders, you probably initially want to simplify it and be very directed and specific in your language as to how people put their hands together and create the knot (start and stop signals). You might also want to "guarantee" that the solution is going to happen, by shrinking the groups to four or five people. This will minimize frustration and blaming and make the kids more willing to try again. We might play this out at one more level. Suppose you were in two feet of pool water with this fourth grade group. (Knots is a wonderful game in the water.) You would obviously have to maintain more vigilance in terms of safety because this is a potential life or death situation. It also means that you would need to be outside the group observing, whereas in many groups playing knots, you can be part of the group and still be a leader.

Another View on Situational Leadership: Hersey and Blanchard's Model

Before closing out this section and giving you some situational problem-solving exercises, we would be remiss if we didn't tell you more about another approach to situational leadership, by two other world renowned experts on leadership. Hersey and Blanchard's model of situational leadership complements all of what we've just said as well as emphasizing some additional factors that you as an advanced leader should take into account when planning and leading your play experiences.

The Theories

Simply put, the play leader should be aware of the readiness and development level of the group members ("relationship" behavior) and their ability level to carry out the "task" (in this case, their ability to play a particular game or engage in a problem-solving initiative activity). As a leader you should ask:

> How tight is the group? How mature are its members? How well do they trust each other and how well will they support each other in matters of communication, of silliness, of expressiveness, of risk taking, of safety? How long have they been together? What game might be appropriate for their level of readiness? What sequence of activities might help them become more cohesive? How much tellling versus selling versus participating versus delegating should you do with your group? What percentage of directive and/or supportive leadership should you use? How much coaching will they need?

In *Leisure Leadership* Niepoth (1983, p. 145) further explains Hersey and Blanchard's theory this way:

> The basic premise of the theory is that with immature individuals or groups, the most effective leadership approach will be a mix of high-task and low-relationship behaviors. As the maturity of the individual or group increases, the effective leader will increase relationship behaviors, and decrease task behaviors. With further increases in maturity, the leader also decreases relationship behaviors. With a highly mature individual or group, the most effective leadership style will be low in both task and relationship behaviors.

While we do not completely agree with the last sentence (we believe in the importance of ongoing strong relationship behavior), the Hersey and Blanchard model is still very useful to us in many ways. For example, if your

play group is not very mature, you would want to be more precise with the
rules and explanations and make sure that your classroom or playground organization scheme was tight (e.g., where to stand, start and stop signals, ways
of organizing squads, attention and focus devices). You might also ask what
is the risk (physical or psychological) in any particular activity. If the risk is
high that someone might get "hurt," you must be more directive and present
with high levels of supervision, control, and backup. As your group and individuals grow in their maturity (and you can help make that happen), they will
become more capable of organizing themselves, making up and changing
rules, mediating disputes, and monitoring *most* safety issues.

Niepoth (1983, p. 147) elaborates:

> This means that the ability to analyze and diagnose situations, and
> the ability to make accurate inferences about the feelings, expecta-
> tions, and capabilities of group members are both necessary prereq-
> uisites to effective leadership. It also means that leaders must be able
> to adapt their styles to varying circumstances. This is not easy—we
> tend to find a particular method of leading and use it consistently,
> usually one with which we had initial success. Also, some styles of
> leadership tend to be more comfortable and natural for us than oth-
> ers. The challenge is to adapt appropriately to meet the demands of
> changing situations without violating our basic personality struc-
> tures—that is, without "trying to be persons that we're not." Part of
> the challenge is to be more open to ways of growing and changing
> that will permit us to be more adaptable.
>
> Changes in style should not be made for the sake of change alone.
> Enough consistency in style is needed so that those with whom the
> leader works will know what to expect, and not be confused. Modifi-
> cations in style are called for when the circumstances change within
> which the leader is working, and when the leader's current approach
> is ineffective. Also, it's possible that a leader may not be effective in
> some situations, regardless of the style he or she selects. The objec-
> tive in adapting to circumstances is to maximize one's effective-
> ness—to become as effective as possible and to change when
> appropriate. However, temporary setbacks or failures to achieve ob-
> jectives may not be causes for change. Sensitivity is required in de-
> termining when to continue with an approach and when to modify it.
>
> As suggested in Hersey and Blanchard's theories, the leader may,
> depending upon the circumstances, select a style that gives greater or
> lesser emphasis to task-oriented and relationship-oriented behaviors.
> However, this doesn't mean that, in situations where there is a rela-

tively greater focus on task-oriented behaviors, the leader can ignore completely the matter of interpersonal relationships. A leader's emphasis on the task need not be carried out in ways that alienate or threaten members.

Remember the game (task) is only the structure that allows us to play. The goal is always the facilitation and maintenance of that spirit of playfulness and Flow (Big Fun) and moving with the group toward greater levels of empowerment and democracy. The tricky thing is to analyze and start where the group "is at," to be adaptable and yet genuine. Since Hersey and Blanchard's original model there have been many modifications and variations developed by Blanchard and others. Many of these are detailed in Johnson and Johnson (1997) and the reader is invited to further explore these. You can't get too much information on group theory, process, and dynamics.

Some Problem Solving

What is important about all these different examples is that by fine tuning and adapting your situational leadership approach you can come up with a way to safely allow the group to truly play. Here are a few examples you might encounter in your play leadership career. Consider these exercises. Jot down key words that target your artful responses.

What Would You Do?

- Suppose you have just explained a long and complicated game such as Ultimate Frisbee. You have two more things you need to let people know and they are really antsy and ready to play and all of a sudden, 30 new people walk up and say, "Hey, how do you play this game?" What would you do?

- Suppose you just started to begin a session of Knots and lo and behold, out of the minivan that has just pulled up, three people in wheelchairs enthusiastically disembark and ask if they can join in the game? What would you do?

- Suppose you have 25 school kids out for field day to play games in a large grassy park, when all of a sudden it begins to rain with accompanying thunder and lightning, just enough so that you think the little ones might get frizzled. Your only opportunity to find an indoor space is to go into the nearby park museum which has a 12-by-14-foot small room. What would you do?

- Suppose you have a very active, energetic group and you've been having a great time playing a lot of running around games, and during a particularly lively game of British Bulldog (a rugby-type game), one of the people in the group makes the wrong move at the right time and sprains her ankle very severely. What would you do?

- Suppose you're at a banquet with 300 people, all of whom are sitting at long tables. After dinner they are listening to speakers, and the first two have been particularly long-winded and boring. Knowing that there are three more speakers to go, the Master of Ceremonies realizes that this group needs to be energized and asks you to lead a game. What would you do?

By the way, to get the most out of this exercise, you should in fact, at this very moment, go into your darkened closet with 200 Nerf balls and someone you love (other than yourself). One of you should be dressed in a three-piece suit, and the other in a scuba outfit. Proceed to explore the game of Dodge Ball. After you've come up with 10 different ways to play Dodge Ball in that situation and setting with that group of players, then, we think, you're primed to fully explore what you would do in the situations mentioned here. (Don't forget to go back and think them through...we're watching you.) What other situations can you share with your fellow play leaders that will help all of you in your ongoing growth?

Discipline

Kids are like a wet bar of soap—you hold them too tight, you lose them...you hold them too loose, you lose them.

—Anonymous

In our experience we have very rarely had any "discipline" problems with adult players that a quick huddle and reminder couldn't solve (usually that reminder is about paying more attention to physical or emotional safety). We've worked enough in the real world to know that is not always the case with kids. They are still discovering that interplay between freedom and behavioral boundaries and as play leaders we can be a big help in their growth. In this whole book we've been emphasizing how important it is to encourage freedom, empowerment and creativity, and to be positive and enthusiastic about our programs. But it is also true that no matter how well-thought-out our program is, kids still need guidance boundaries and direction and yes, *sometimes,* "sanctions."

Ours is a three-pronged approach to discipline. It involves (a) a broad-based approach to creating positive behavior, (b) general principles of discipline, and (c) what to do when all else fails (including principles and steps of assertive discipline and a menu of problem-solving sanctions and solutions). This also includes things not to do. Discipline should not be seen as negative. At its best it's self-control and self-responsibility. The most powerful discipline is a highly motivating program with a lot of choices and enthusiastic leaders that are good models for, and respected by, their groups. Although there may be sometimes that you'll need to use assertive discipline leadership techniques, the best approach is positive reinforcement. Think of the many ways that you can encourage and reinforce positive attitudes and actions. We know of programs that have a "leader of the week" program (that rotates to different kids). Another program has a "catch of the day" program where the leaders catch a kid being good and reward that behavior. Find ways to encourage self-respect and responsibility and other *values* through both systems and activity themes (e.g., how do we show *caring* through art or games?). Help kids know that positive behavior is important not just because you get an M&M but because *it's the right thing to do*.

Approaches to Positive Behavior

Probably 90% of discipline "problems" can be prevented by *front-end loading*. That is by asking yourself what kids need and then having your program, leadership, learning environment, and expectations respond to those needs.

What Kids Need

A couple of acronyms remind us of some basics. The first is the four Ls of childhood:

- *Love*. To be cared about; affection, warmth, appreciation.

- *Liberty*. Within limits, the freedom to choose, to be successful, to be expressive, to make mistakes, to learn responsibility, and to accept the consequences of behavior; to not be "overprogrammed."

- *Limits*. Behavioral boundaries, expectations, and rules.

- *Listen*. Actively listen to what kids are saying to you by their words or deeds. They have a lot to say and can teach us a lot.

Our expanded version of Denny McClaughlin's ARRRFF principle overlaps and expands on some key elements of self-esteem and happiness kids need:

- *Achievement*. Help kids accomplish and learn new things; they are building blocks of self-esteem.

- *Respect*. For self, others, equipment, supplies, and the facility.

- *Responsibility*. No matter what kids' personal circumstances may be they are responsible for their actions.

- *Resourcefulness*. How can we help kids realize and maximize the resources within them and around them (e.g., to change games, create scrap art projects, and be responsible for their own fun and excitement versus being media dependent).

- *Freedom* (aka, "liberty") to choose, to grow, to say no or yes to stretch, to just be a kid.

- *Fun*. Don't we all need and want it in our work and play?

If we build our programs (and leadership styles) around the four Ls and the ARRRFF principle we'll go a long way toward eliminating most of our discipline problems.

For example, if we give kids *choices* in our program (and) flexibly "overplan" accordingly, we pay attention to the kids' needs for freedom (liberty). No matter how good our one idea may have been (according to us), the kids might not like it and might act out in negative ways. By providing a menu of choices or the flexibility to change the game or the rules we head off some potential discipline problems. A few other questions to consider:

- In what ways are we defining limits and behavioral boundaries in our programs?

- How are we helping kids achieve (e.g., learning to catch a ball, draw a face)?

- What ways are we teaching respect plus responsibility (e.g., do we have "fair play" rules; are the kids helping us lead the games and pick up the equipment)? Does everyone get a chance to be the "referee"?

- Are we helping kids be resourceful by inventing games, coming up with rules and changes?

- Is our program fun and are we listening to what kids think is fun?

Another Look at Front-End Loading

Another broad-based approach to creating positive behavior is to have your staff sit down and identify the ways you are creating positive behavior in three areas: (a) the environment (both physical and psychological), (b) the program and leadership, and (c) your reasonable behavioral expectations from the kids, including an agreed on consistent sequence of dealing with misbehavior. Again, a few examples and questions will illustrate this approach:

- *Environment, Physical.* What are the colors in your center (are they bright, stimulating)? Are there quiet spaces? Are the kids' materials actively displayed on the wall? Are there soft spaces, living things (plants), sounds? Have you structured your room to eliminate potential discipline problems. We know of a childcare center that put a learning center in the middle of an open room and eliminated a "running" problem.

- *Environment, Psychological.* Is there an atmosphere of warmth, caring, empowerment, and inclusion? How are kids picked for games? Have elimination activities been eliminated? How are the kids greeted and thanked at the beginning and end of your program?

- *Program (and Leadership).* What about choices, variety, developmental appropriateness, and responsiveness to kids needs, themes? Good humanistic leadership training?

- *Expectations and Dealing With Misbehavior.* What are the three to five "rules" that are absolutely important for the kids and the smooth operation of the program? What are the steps your staff will take to enforce them (e.g., three strikes and you're out; two verbal warnings)? Have a plan. Can you state most of them in ways that express the positive behavior you want (e.g., "use quiet inside voices" vs. "no yelling").

The previous are but a few examples of approaches to front-end loading. The point is that if you or your staff take the time to pay attention to the kids' needs and to analyze how every aspect of your program can feed into positive behavior, you'll go a long way toward eliminating 90% of your discipline problems.

Some General Principles of Positive Discipline

Remember this variation of Baldwin's five Cs of discipline with LASERBEAMS:

1. *Caring*. Even though a child is being disciplined for an inappropriate action he or she should always know he or she is cared about as a person. And tomorrow is a clean slate. This is easier said than done because we often stereotype our troublemakers, jump too fast when they act up, and don't see them doing anything positive.

2. *Consistent*. We should strive toward consistency in our approaches to discipline (e.g., rules enforcement) even though we must know and recognize children as individuals and individualize approaches when appropriate (e.g., some kids need a more "direct" approach, while others respond better to more quiet huddles and counseling). There should not be sets of rules for the goody-two-shoes and the difficult kids. Also staff must be consistent in their enforcement of rules (so kids don't get mixed messages and/or play staff against each other).

3. *Communication*. What is it (i.e., the positive behaviors) that you expect of the children? How do you communicate that (verbally, with signs, with songs or rituals)? If you don't communicate what you want, how will they know?

4. *Choices*. If we are to raise responsible children they should know that they have choices as to how they act. They choose and are responsible for their actions. This doesn't mean that we don't care (or cry inside) about circumstances that they may come from that may influence anger, aggression, and acting out. Hitting is still not appropriate.

5. *Consequences*. Children also need to know that there are consequences to their behaviors—both good and bad—and most often depending on the choices they make. Which leads to our next acronym, LASERBEAMS:

   - **L**ook for
   - **A**ny
   - **S**igns of
   - **E**ncourageable

- **R**einforceable
- **B**ehavior so that
- **E**xpectations
- **A**re
- **M**otivated
- **S**uccessfully

In other words, "Catch 'em being good!"—which happens to be the title of one of our favorite discipline books. Catch kids doing the positive things you want them to and reinforce it—verbally (Wow!), nonverbally (a pat on the back) or through many other behavioral "systems" (more about that later). Create positive conspiracies with other staff so that problem kids will have a positive experience, get attention for that, and perhaps begin to learn a new way to be in the world. In fact how many verbal and nonverbal ways can you think of to tell a child that he or she did a good job! Brainstorm at least 20 (e.g., high-fives; say, "awesome").

Some other general principles and techniques of positive discipline:

1. Highlight the behavior not the child ("That was an inappropriate action" *not* "You stupid kid"). Even though a child has done some thing wrong, and been disciplined, the child should know that he or she is still liked.

2. Keep your discipline and routines tighter at first. Then relax them if appropriate as you get to know your kids. The reverse is almost impossible.

3. One of the best preventative techniques is to let the kids know right up front that there are certain expectations, limits, and boundaries and specific consequences or sanctions if the boundaries are crossed. Let them know the reason for these (e.g., health, safety). If possible, try to get the kids to "buy in" and suggest or agree on some basic understandings. It may seem cruel to "read 'em the rules" right at the beginning. After all, the program is supposed to be fun! But, one of the biggest difficulties with discipline is not being clear about expectations and arbitrarily making up rules as you go along. Be sure to be upbeat about positive expectations about the program and their behavior. Try also to practice stating expectations in *positive language* (e.g., "please walk" vs. "don't run," "speak softly, please" versus "don't yell," "be careful of other children" vs. "don't run into other kids").

4. New leaders, especially, are often concerned that they will not be seen as a "fun person" if they bring up expectations and rules too early in their contact with the kids. Be assured that there is no contradiction between being an enthusiastic, positive, fun leader and enforcing the rules.

5. Be consistent, be evenhanded (fair), and follow-up where it is appropriate (especially if you say you're going to take an action—otherwise don't say it).

6. Let the child express his or her feelings, but remain calm and stay on track regarding what you want from him or her. If you can, deal with a child's problems one-on-one, in private, separate from the group. Don't hold kids up to ridicule.

7. Be serious when you need to be, but never lose your sense of humor and perspective. Children's play programs are supposed to be fun for everyone (including leaders) and even though we will all give it our best shot there may be some rare kid's behavior that just might not be changed the way we would like it to be in our time together. Kids may bring a lot of emotional "baggage" or difficult circumstances with them to your program. Try to understand it and do your best to exercise the five Cs. This is also a reminder of our need to be ongoing advocates for social justice and to partner with other community agencies and professionals that can assist us (e.g., counseling folks, juvenile diversion).

8. Use good group-building, attention-getting, and quiet down, stress-reduction techniques. These are "creative control" methods and have a lot to do with discipline and positive behavior. They help to avoid trying to yell at the top or your lungs over 45 active kids, they help to avoid tug-of-war power trips (win–lose) and they pay attention to real needs (as opposed to symptoms). After all don't we *all* need relaxation and quiet areas in our lives? For example, Bill has often had kids lie on the floor, do some deep breathing and do a guided visualization where they imagine themselves in a quiet, special space. He also knows a preschool teacher who uses a "soft blue box" when her kids' energy seems to get out of hand negatively. Each child has a soft blue box (with soft blue objects in it) to play with and change the "energy." Soothing music can also be used to help provoke the quieting response.

    Another example was when Bill was working with first grade kids and they were crashing into each other in a movement activity.

He had them imagine themselves with a giant bubble around them, and if they crashed, the bubble would pop and they would sit for a couple of minutes. Kids wanted to move and play so they stopped crashing (mostly).

9. Use positive peer pressure: Identify leaders or lightning rods in your group and use them as your ally (e.g., "Could you help me carry the ball bag?" or "Could you help me get this game going?").

10. Use a "leader of the week" button (a special helper).

11. Have weekly meetings with kids to check in with them about how they are doing regarding the "rules," their needs, and how they are cooperating.

12. Do short-term huddles or "temperature readings" individually or collectively. Are you 98.6° or 104°? What can you do about it? Also use a team approach and pull one kid aside while your partner continues to lead the game. Tell the kid that you value him or her as a player but that hitting or pushing is "out of bounds" and that you expect that he or she will play fair and safely. If this doesn't work after huddling a couple of times, you'll have to show you do mean business and impose a sanction.

13. Engage in good teamwork with your staff and "spell" each other (help each other out). Have a consistent plan of how you all will approach Jimmy's hitting so that he doesn't play one side against the other. Recognize that you're going to have good and bad days so take a time-out yourself while one of your coworkers is the more high-visibility leader.

14. Use catharsis activities (boffers, punching bags) and/or redirect the energy appropriately. The kids may need to run around the block, or they may need to breathe, do yoga, or do a calming art actively to music. See your activities as tools to help kids grow.

15. Try using a buddy system where you pair kids up so they might be able to model desirable behavior and teach each other.

16. Change the game (or activity). Sometimes a quick rules change will prevent people from crashing into each other and provide more success, and you've headed off frustration and confrontation.

17. Try to distinguish between the behavior and what it might really mean. For example, a lot of kids act out in negative ways to say,

"Look at me, I'm someone! Pay attention to me!" or "I'm sad or angry or hurting and I just haven't found a way to deal with that." This doesn't mean that we can ignore the behavior, but we're challenged to get beyond the surface manifestations and find other ways to give that child attention (and gradually mold more "positive" actions) or use activities and strategies that help the child to cope with that hurt or anger. Caring is at the top of the five Cs list.

18. It's also important not to overreact to every perceived "infraction" that kids do. Many behaviors can and will be extinguished if they are simply ignored or not validated (e.g., yelling for attention). If it's an unsuccessful strategy, kids will often abandon it (especially if we show them a more successful one). For example, studies have shown that male loudness and aggressiveness tends to be overly attended to and reinforced in early childhood settings, thereby leading to the self-fulfilling prophecy that boys are "naturally" louder and more aggressive. Pick your battles and remember what it was like to be a fourth grader. (How many of you still have trouble with impulse control?)

19. Back to positive reinforcement. There are a lot of systems that can be used to reinforce observed positive behavior. These can be successful in some contexts but have limitations and should never be the only approach to discipline. Nor should they substitute for flexible, sensitive leadership or stressing that behaving is important because it's the right thing to do. Many programs are using character education or values curricula to reinforce the importance of such core values as respect, responsibility and caring. A couple of positive reinforcement systems examples are (a) stars or stickers next to a kid's name on an individual card and (b) macaroni jars where each kid has his own jar and gets a macaroni put in it when he or she does a positive behavior. There are endless variations of these. Our bias is to not use a comparison chart (kids should be compared to their own behavior and how it stacks up to clearly defined "expectations"). Some centers "auction" or give away "miniprizes" (kept in perspective) when a child has earned so many macaronis. The important thing is to have a comprehensive positive behavior and discipline program. We won't always have macaroni jars (or M&Ms) with us in life, although initial external "rewards" can help to shape behavior and values.

If All Else Fails

So what if all else fails? You've tried all of these suggestions and Louie (or Louise) is still running around hitting people. First, once again take a deep breath and remind yourself that it's an imperfect world (this is momentarily consoling), and that kids as fellow travelers on the planet are trying to figure it out (rules, boundaries, freedom, expressiveness, control sanctions) just like us (without our years of experience and wisdom). The important thing to remember is that you have a right to respect (which must be mutual) and a right to run a fun, healthy, and safe program. Kids testing rules and boundaries are a normal part of socialization. As a staff member you will need a wide range of strategies in your repetoire, everything from providing more choices, to redirecting, to parent conferences, to expulsion from the program. In addition to what is in this chapter, *Kids Time Manual* and Dale Fink's book (all listed in Chapter 12, *Resources, Connections, and Beyond*) have excellent charts and suggestions on the range of successful strategies needed.

There are a lot of "sanctions," some better than others and some definitely not good. Each has its own strengths and shortcomings, and should be used in the context of all of the these suggestions for positive behavior. These "sanctions" are followed by the principles and steps of assertive discipline. It's our strong belief that assertive discipline principles and procedures should be followed as a regular part of your discipline and positive behavior program and certainly used as you are going to impose sanctions.

Sanctions

1. *At Arm's Length (Time-In)*. The child must follow you around and be within arm's length at all time. "You've shown me that you're not capable of controlling yourself and therefore you'll be with me until..." (This is generally not fun for either party but gives you the opportunity to talk and explore issues.)

2. *Physical Distance*. Children want to play or be part of the action (or be close enough to disrupt the action). Removing a child far away from the action (yet still within a visual supervision) can isolate the child's negative power and often be effective.

3. *Lose an Activity* (e.g., lose a day or week of swimming). This can be combined with any of the others. See #6 on p. 149 for shortcomings of this.

4. ***Time-Outs***. These generally should be short (a few minutes) in du-
   ration. Time-outs also can be used as a preventative measure for
   kids to rest, to sit, to be in a quiet soft place before things really get
   out of hand. Generally the best approach to time-outs is to put the
   responsibility back on the child (e.g., "Come back when you're
   ready to play without hitting or pushing."). Time-outs are usually
   more effective when combined with physical distance. If you don't
   like the concept of time-out, call it "Rest and Reflect." Better yet,
   create a "balance center" with various activities that aid the reflection and redirection of the child (and help restore balance) or a
   "peace table" with ground rules for cooling off, discussion and me-
   diation.

5. ***Respectful Negotiations and Behavioral Contracts***. Discussing
   issues, listing the desired behavior positive reinforcements and
   "sanctions" mutually agreed on, signed by key people, and
   monitored regularly. Contracts can be verbal or written.

6. ***Unexpected Surprise Consequences***. Post-it notes that blow their
   cover (e.g., "You could have been louder in line today.") or if they
   were loud, have them lead a quiet activity the next day.

7. ***Logical Consequences Related to Their Behavior***. If they never
   pick up, their job is to use their free period to clean up the center,
   or if they break stuff, their job is to repair toys. Logical consequences are generally the *best* first approach when all else fails.

8. ***Peer Counseling and Conflict Resolution***. This is being used more
   and more where a trained group of children and/or leaders work
   with the "offender" to identify and to mediate solutions and/or
   sanctions. But more importantly, do extensive preventative work.
   Children as Peacemakers and the Second Step programs have extensive resource catalogs in this area. The less we can "rescue"
   children (by making quick, authoritative judgements) and the more
   we help kids help themselves, the better off we will all be. We
   know a program that has a simple acronym, TAG, where they
   teach kids in conflict: *Tell* the person what the problem is and what
   you would like him or her to do about it. *Ask* the person to cooper-
   ate on alternative solutions. *Get* help from an adult to mediate the
   problem. Many national programs are teaching young kids
   assertiveness language. We need to start early in giving kids verbal
   problem solving skills (versus violence and aggression). See *Adventures in Peacemaking—A Conflict Resolution Guide for School-
   Age Programs* for 200-plus strategies.

Some Bad (Abusive and Ineffective in the Long Run) Ways to Discipline

1. ***Punishing the whole group for something one person did***. This only turns the group against that individual and further isolates him or her.

2. ***Using physical punishment*** (e.g., laps, push-ups). We are about teaching children to love themselves, their bodies, wellness, games, and play. Using physical punishment is the opposite message (i.e., activity is associated not with positive fitness or wellness but with pain and negativity). There are also serious legalities and liabilities here.

3. ***Writing "I must not..." sentences***. Again writing should be seen as a part of positive learning.

4. ***Calling kids out in front of the whole group***. Sometimes it can't be totally avoided but try your best to pull the kid aside while your coleader (or student leader) handles the group.

5. ***Downgrading kids and/or comparing them to others*** (versus their own behavior and the program's expectations). "You stupid idiot!" "I'll kill you!" or "Why can't you be like your sister. I had her in the program a couple of years ago."

6. ***Always restricting or removing play as a punishment***. Of course play is a powerful part of kids' lives. That is why we adults use it as both a carrot ("clean up your room and you get an extra half-hour of TV") and a stick ("you kids have been noisy; there'll be no recess") to try to mold children's behavior. The real danger here is that play will be seen as not a natural behavior (which it is) but something very fragile that must be earned or deferred until all the "important" (work) things are done. Play is indeed an important way children learn and exist in the world. Ultimately the carrot-and-stick approach reinforces our cultures' guilt and anxiety about play, work, and leisure issues and leads to time-scarce, highly stressed adults who have not been able to integrate or balance their lives. Use the other "if all else fails" methods.

A couple of other things to mention. First, use common sense and let the sanction be in proportion with the "crime." Second, as a leader don't be afraid to seek additional support (from your coworkers or superiors) before you even get to the sanctions stage. This is not a sign of weakness, but a sign of strength. You do not have to be continually miserable or frustrated because one needy kid is continually acting out. Also remember the other 35 children that you are in charge of deserve a good program too. *But don't write off that problem kid, because you could be the one to turn him or her around.*

Effective Communication: Assertive Discipline, "I" Messages, and Limited Choice Language

Simply put, assertiveness is the use of "I" statements to express your feelings, to own your opinions, and ultimately to get your needs met. It's an essential part of any play leader's discipline approach. It's very important for the leader to know the difference between assertive, nonassertive, and hostile–aggressive style of discipline and communication. A *nonassertive style* says you want to be loved so much that you'll let the kids walk all over you. In fact, if they want to burn the building down, you are likely to give them the matches. While the kids might say you're cool (in the short run) for cutting them slack, in the long run it won't work and leads to chaos. A *hostile* or *aggressive style* personalizes everything the kids do wrong and attempts to use size, strength, loudness, screaming, and intimidation to control behavior (e.g., "I don't get paid enough to put up with what you do to me," "Get out of my face, you low-life dog!" or "Give me 50 push-ups, you idiot"). While this may seem cathartic or effective in the short run, it only raises blood pressure, shuts down communication, and alienates everyone (leading to fight or flight). Sure, if you are six-feet, three-inches tall and weigh 200 pounds, you can scare a sixth grader, but it's not what we are about nor is it effective in the long run in terms of helping people grow in positive directions. And it's abusive. And believe it or not it gives the child tremendous power to push your buttons (and in fact enlist others to help launch you through the ceiling). The only alternative is *assertiveness*, which says, as mentioned earlier, that you the have right of mutual respect, and the right to run a fun, safe, healthy program. Assertiveness lets you state how you feel and what you want from the child. You own your own feelings and do not create or reinforce a codependent situation with the child where he or she is in charge of your feelings (see our tips for successful "I" messages).

"I" statements do work if you practice. They focus you, keep you on track, and keep the communication lines open while you say how you feel and what you want. They are the only long-range effective way to get your needs and the kids' needs met. Knowing and using the assertiveness formula will not only make you a better, more effective play leader, it's a generic life skill that can be applied to all of your relationships. And it makes for less stress, more human dignity, and ultimately more fun.

Successful "I" Messages

Assertiveness Formula =   <u>I feel</u>   <u>when</u>   <u>because</u>   and   <u>I want.</u>
                           A   B   C   D

Or

When you _____ I feel _____ because
_____ and I want (or need or would like) _____.

Guidelines for successful "I" messages

- When stating *A,* state a feeling, not a claim. "I feel that you're a jerk," is an attack statement, not an "I" statement. The word "that" is a clue that you are not stating a feeling.

- When stating *B,* try not to use the word "you." "You" creates a feeling of blame and sets up defensiveness in whoever you are disciplining. The truth is, you would resent this behavior from anyone, not just this person.

- "I" statements should also be used (mostly) with positive behaviors. ("I feel great when older kids stay with the group because it's a model for the younger kids. I want you to keep doing that.")

Sample situation

It is one of your camper's responsibility to pick up the play equipment immediately after your games session. It is quite a bit later and the equipment isn't picked up yet.

Sample "I" message

"I feel angry when the equipment isn't picked up on time because it bothers me to have an unsafe unsupervised area where the equipment might get ripped off. I want the equipment picked up now."

Sample situation

One of your students has been trying to diet and another student makes sarcastic jokes about her weight.

Sample "I" message

"I feel sad when someone jokes about someone's weight because it is embarrassing. I want other people's problems to be taken seriously."

Limited Choice Language

The other communication technique regarding discipline in play leadership situations is learning how to become effective in using limited choice language. *Limited choice language* gives the child the dignity of some behavioral choices within your play context (versus screaming at him or her, "Don't touch this...don't touch that") and it puts the responsibility for the behavior choice back on the child where it belongs. For example: "You can throw the Frisbee on the grass or on the playground but not in the class. Where do *you* want to throw the Frisbee?" *Not* "I'd prefer if you'd throw the Frisbee on the grass" (*too much* wiggle room).

After presenting the choices make sure you ask the child, "What would you like to do?" This places the responsibility for making the decision on the child's shoulders. Don't continue to repeat the choice (more than three times [see the following]). If the child states that he or she will comply but continues to violate the choice then it is most likely time for that fifth C: consequences. Remember to pick your battles. Be assured that the combination of assertiveness and limited choice language are powerful tools that respect people and yet guide behavior in the direction you want.

Steps of Assertive Discipline

The following are recommended steps in implementing assertive discipline:

- Give an active response: approval or disapproval of behavior, rules, violations.

- Make eye contact. Eye contact is generally very important as is "leveling" with the child (bending or stooping down so you're eye-to-eye) but keep in mind cross-cultural differences regarding eye contact. In an Anglo culture the "eyes are the mirror of the soul" and eye contact by the disciplined child is seen as a sign of respect ("look at me when I'm talking to you"), whereas in some cultures, eyes down is the respectful gesture. The important thing is to read the child's total body language to see if he or she is "with you" and is comprehending your message.

- Call the child's name.

- Make an assertive, calm, needs statement; do limit setting (tell what you want from child), showing firmness and conviction. Your tone is important here. Do not keep it light, frilly, and playful. That will send a mixed message that you are maybe not serious. Also do not be the yelling, intimidating tyrant.

- Use a gesture or touch if appropriate (e.g., hand on shoulder). The leader again should be sensitive to the hostility of the situation and cross-cultural differences. Sometimes a gesture or touch acts as a "connection" (I'm here, I'm serious) and sometimes it's better to allow more space and not get in someone's face. Being "in touch" can sometimes escalate the situation.

- Use repetition or the broken record technique ("that's not the point..." or "I understand, but I still need you to get out of the pool"). After about three requests the situation becomes a mind game, power trip, tug of war (and you want to avoid that). To repeat, it's better to discipline in private (or in one-and-one huddles) if possible. It avoids the "Days of Our Lives" drama, where everyone is looking to see who "wins."

- State your consequences (if appropriate).

- Follow through (as needed).

- Seek additional support (if necessary).

Two further suggestions to implement assertive discipline are:

- Use active listening-feedback loops and/or questioning strategies to make sure that everyone is on track (e.g., "What's the rule for snack time, Susie?" [questioning strategy] or "What I hear you saying, Mikey, is that you are clear about the playground rules" [active listening feedback loop]).

- Use yes/no questions to vague responses if necessary (e.g., "Did you push Zelmo down?").

There are no miracles in discipline, no automatic formulas that will guarantee you 100% success or magically transform a superneedy kid into an angel. But all of the previously mentioned principles of discipline and developing positive behavior do work if you work at them. You'll get better at it, more confident, less stressed, and you truly can help meet the needs of a wide range of children and help them grow. The kids need you and behavioral boundaries.

The biggest mistakes in discipline situations are:

1. not being assertive

2. being overly strict or rigid

3. being overly permissive

4. being inconsistent

5. voicing threats and downgrading kids

6. comparing kids to other kids rather than to their own behavior

7. not allowing kids to express their own feelings

8. not having a positive attitude and upbeat expectations

Finally, in summary, remember and act on the word PEACEFUL (and your play leader life will be much more that way):

- **P**ositive reinforcement

- **E**xpectations

- **A**ssertiveness

- **C**aring, Consistent, Communication, Choices, Consequences

- **E**venhanded

- **F**ollow-up

- **U**pbeat

- **L**ove, Liberty, Limits, Listen and LASERBEAMS

...ARRRFF! (Good job!)

...End of Discipline Section. Thanks for being disciplined.

Advanced Leadership Skills: A Summary

The challenge for you as an advanced leader is to continually take risks and to expose yourself to a wide range of groups, situations, and settings; to expand your repertoire of games and techniques; to move beyond this to intuitively explore new dimensions of playfulness; and to fine tune your practical application of discipline principles, empowerment, Flow, and situational leadership theory. This is a lifelong quest and all of this will contribute to your sensitivities and the *Art of Your Play Leadership*. Stay at it!

However, if you don't want to wait that long (like the rest of your life) to get good at this, or to put in the requisite amount of time, energy, and effort that it takes to be an artist, for a mere $200 and a self-addressed, stamped, big envelope, we'll be glad to send the Advanced Referee Kit. This includes Gucci Shoes, the Advanced Referee Skills T-Shirt, and Bubblegum Cards of all the Advanced Referees in the World, plus an official certification certificate certifying that, indeed, you've been certified... (Just fooling...)

Chapter 9

A Bigger Bag of Tricks

It takes such a long time to grow young and I'm only now just getting the hang of it.

—Picasso (at 80)

Throughout this book we've listed a lot of hints for making your leadership more refined, more three-dimensional. Here are a few more. In fact, this chapter might be called *The Book of Lists, Part II*. We've also tried to be clear that in the play leadership business there are no "formulas," but nevertheless we've found that some of these "lists" have proven to be useful—or at the very least mildly amusing to us (so don't blame us—besides you've been sworn to secrecy with this highly classified information).

We encourage you to develop your own "lists" and your own playbook and to constantly seek out new resources as part of your ongoing growth as a play leader. This includes connecting with key people, organizations, publications, and conferences and haunting new and especially used bookstores. (The best resources are often found here and at flea markets, garage sales, and thrift stores.) This resource development also involves asking the kids and/or your other players for their knowledge. Remember, games are a form of folklore that come from many sources and go through cycles of "visibility." (For example, did you know that the game Pictionary is over 100 years old?) Some of your best sources of fun may be old social recreation activities and parlor games. Chapter 12, *Resources, Connections, and Beyond*, will say a lot more about resources.

Five (or More) "Openers" That the Pros Use

In addition to the invitation–permission activities and warmups mentioned in Chapter 3, *Getting It Going*, there are a few other "can't miss" games that we like to use to begin play sessions or events, depending on the players' situation and setting. Think through what you want to accomplish and how you can set up *all* the elements of the play experience for success.

Most often when we open we want to let people know, "This is play" (we're playing for the fun of it), and we want to get them interacting and involved (using mixers, icebreakers, and name games) without being too obtrusive (still letting them ease in). Remember, it's an "opening" general principle to start with more familiar activities or variations of them and move gradually to greater levels of intimacy by introducing newer (and perhaps

...ige or potentially "threatening") activities as the group becomes more comfortable. In other words, don't start out with an "eyes closed" game where people have to do a lot of touching and bark like dogs! With all that in mind, some of our favorite games we've liked to open with are Elbow Tag, Last Detail, People to People, Group Juggle, Instant Replay, Everybody Is It Tag, and Pile Up. All of these can be found in *More New Games* and/or many other spin-off books derived from it. A few others (with detail) that we've enjoyed opening with include:

Wordles. Individual or team word puzzles (e.g., you/just/me = just between you and me). These can be found in *Silver Bullets, Games* magazine and in puzzle books.

15-Second Handshake Variations. ("Hi, my name is..."; shaking hands with as many people as you can in 30 seconds.) Try different handshake variations (e.g., left handed and funny shakes).

The Wind Blows. People in circular or semicircular formation; "caller" calls out a "quality" (e.g., white shoes) that anyone in the circle might have: "The wind blows people with white shoes on." They must exchange seats with others who have that quality while the caller also tries to get a seat. The one without a seat is the leader of the next round. Encourage safety and strategies that don't allow anyone to feel foolish or isolated for long (e.g., "everyone who is wearing clothing" exchange seats—this gives the person a chance to get a chair). Also encourage the leader to introduce himself or herself and for the group to welcome and applaud him or her.

Partnering Techniques. These are great for generating energy and helping people to make connections. For example, have people find a high-five partner. The two people then slap high-fives five times while simultaneously saying each other's names. Try Leaping Double High-Fives Partners or Do-Si-Do Partners using the same principle. (What other ways can you think of?) Remember the "rule of three" when asking to get partners (so no one gets left out or feels anxious about getting left out). If someone doesn't find a partner in three seconds, they can be part of a group of threes (so pairs *or* threes are OK).

Cooperative Rock, Paper, Scissors Variations. Essentially a pair of people attempting to match the same symbol (e.g., two "rocks" [fists]) after a ritual counting, "One, two, three, throw." After matching, they celebrate by throwing their hands up and cheering, "We did it." Try different sized groups (e.g., threes, fours) and different possibilities of matches (same number of fingers, number of fingers adding up to seven or eleven).

Partner or Group Thumb Wrestling. With the partner version, face your partner and one of you crosses your arms (the other doesn't). Lock hands in thumb wrestling position. Have two "matches" at the same time and have repeat matches. With the group version, any even number of players can participate. They stand in a circle, every *other* player with crossed arms (the other player has his or her arms uncrossed), each holding both neighbors' hands in the traditional thumb wrestling position. Now everyone wrestles, and the confusion of having to wrestle two thumbs at once leads to lots of laughter. Have rematches.

Trashball (aka, Kitchen Sink or Clean up Your Room). Don't have any equipment, but still want to get people going? Divide the play space in half with an equal number on each team occupying their half of the court (or room). Have each person crumble a piece of paper (8-1/2-by-11–inches or really any throwable size); write down a time limit known only to you (up to two minutes). When you say, "Go," the group members must throw their paper balls onto the other team's side. The team with the least amount of paper balls on its side at the end "wins."

Down Under. Have people hold hands and run under a jump rope that is being twined toward them (first in ones, then twos, fours, and so on). If you want, some folks in the chain can close their eyes.

Ten or Fewer "Can't Miss When All Else Fails" Games

There probably is no such thing as a totally "can't miss" game, although over the years we've discovered a few games that seemed to work even when all else was collapsing around us. It's great to always have a few of these in your hip pocket for emergencies.

A can't miss game seems to have a few basic qualities: (1) you like to play it a lot, (2) it involves a lot of folks (it's highly interactive), (3) it has a relatively simple rules structure and can be easily explained, (4) it has a lot of variations, and (5) with a simple twist it works with a wide range of age and ability groups. Many of the previously mentioned openers would also fall into the can't miss category (that is why we start with them!).

A few others that can be found in the *New Games* and *More New Games* books are Quick Line-Up; Rock, Paper, Scissors Tag variations (including Giants, Elves, Wizards); Blob Tag; Zoom variations (Ooh Aah variations); Octopus; Smaug's Jewels; most parachute games; and Snake in the Grass. A couple of the others (with details) include

Tunnel Tag Variations. If you're tagged by the "it" person, you're frozen and can only become unfrozen by someone crawling through your legs (from backside to frontside). If the crawler is tagged, he or she is also frozen and must stand in front of the other frozen person (so the tunnel that needs to be crawled through gets longer). On hard surfaces, vary the unfreezing action (e.g., a person is unfrozen when leapfrogged over or when two unfrozen people do a double high-five over their heads and yell, "Chill out").

Balloon Volleyball. Use eight-inch or larger balloons. Have the group line up with a partner, toe-to-toe, facing each other on a center line. Have the group members sit down on the floor with the bottoms of their shoes touching the bottoms of their partner's shoes and be shoulder-to-shoulder with their teammates. You're now "glued" to that spot. You must keep the soles of your shoes in contact with your former "partner" (who is now on the other team). The object of this game is to hit the balloon over the heads of the members of the other team and have it hit the floor. The members of the other team can lean back and prevent the balloon from hitting the floor by blocking the balloon with their arms or hands to save the balloon, but they cannot lose sole contact with their partners. This team is also trying to hit the balloon over the heads of the opposite team to score a point. The outside boundaries are the outside shoulders of the "outside people" (the people on the ends of each line).

Start with one balloon and play short three- to five-point games and then rematches. This keeps the competition low-key. Add another balloon if you like. Try not to call too many sole violations (loss of connection) unless they are blatantly obvious and give the other team a distinct advantage. Have some extra balloons ready in case your "volleyball" breaks.

Of course, there are a lot more! What are *your* favorite "can't miss" activities?

10+ Somewhat "Cute" and Maybe Even Challenging "Transition" Activities

Typical situations often find us needing to move a group from one area to another without taking forever and at the same time keeping the group relatively focused. Transition activities can also help folks to work on a sense of team or "groupness." Here are a few fun and maybe even developmental ways we've found to accomplish that:

- *Give them a time limit*. You would be amazed how it helps people move when you say, "I need you in a seated circle on the other side of the gym in the next three-and-one-half seconds...Go!" Time limits also help in general when you want people to get into formations.

- *Give them a task to accomplish*. This is another good one often used well in combination with a time limit. For example, give each member of your group a puzzle piece so the group members have to work together to assemble it. Or tell them that in the next three minutes they should be seated in a circle and prepared to sing one of their favorite advertising jingles.

- *Do a Rotating Blind Trust Walk.* Everyone's hands are on the shoulders of the person in front of him or her. The front person's eyes are open; everyone else's eyes are closed. Let the first person have about 30 seconds of leadership, then rotate him or her to the back of the line and close his or her eyes (the second person's eyes are now open and he or she is the leader). Be sure to "spot" for hazards (e.g., sharp corners, trees) so that the blind person doesn't walk into a wall. Go slow enough and encourage good communication (verbal and nonverbal).

- *Do a Partner Trust Walk.* Have people pair up with the front person's eyes closed. The person in the back (with eyes open) has his or her hands on the shoulders of his or her partner and is the driver. The person in front has his or her "bumpers" up (arms in front of him or her, palms out). Go slowly enough and periodically rotate the front and back people. You can also create a car and driver or camera and photographer fantasy around this (see *Silver Bullets*).

- *Do a Mobile Red Light–Green Light.* Send the people that you "catch" back only about five yards.

- *Amoeba.* Have a blindfolded or eyes-closed cluster of 10 to 12 people who are attached in some way (e.g., linked elbows). Have one person with his or her eyes open who is the nucleus leader who guides the group.

- *Do a Choo-Choo Train.* One long line with hands on shoulders. Have them make train sounds.

- *Have them all hang on to something while you move that "something" along.* For example, a long jump rope or a parachute where everyone can grab hold.

- *Give them a challenge.* For example: (a) "You have to get to the other side of the field using five different ways of moving," (b) "You have to *safely* move to the other side of the field in groups of five with one person off the ground," (c) "You all have to be attached by pinkies," (d) "The last group seated against the fence will have to sing an advertising jingle for us *or* take a lap around me!" or (e) if the group has good safety consciousness, you can use blanket carries or 2-by-4 board carries (someone carried on a blanket or board).

- *Give them a focus*. If they must walk in lines once again, give them something on which to focus. For example: (a) sing "Do Wah Ditty;" (b) play mobile Simon Says, or (c) hold up flash cards or any number of fingers and have them yell what they see.

What other ways can you think of to use your transition time for fun group builders?

Three Lesser Known Leader Talents

Unmarketable Skills. You'll never make a lot of money on these, but you'll mildly amuse yourself and those around you. Can you hang a spoon from your nose? Can you do simple corny magic tricks? Can you "separate" your thumb or "crack" your nose? Can you talk like a duck? See the *Totally Useless Skills* book and practice! Every semester that Bill has taught his developmental play class, he has challenged himself to start the first day in some insane way to make the students smile, model "craziness" and communicate that spirit of playfulness. For example, he has used music tapes, "young at heart" meditations, and has given everyone in class a Nerf ball and dared the students to throw at him. There are so many of these unmarketable skills to share with your players and to reinforce a good play spirit (e.g., give yourself a round of applause; give yourself a seal of approval, a Standing *O,* a big hand; give your buddy the lumberjack handshake or the cow handshake [if you don't know what any of these are, make up your own]). These skills add more playfulness to the mix.

Deviousity and Opportunism. There is a fine line between facilitation and manipulation and it depends on whether your heart and motives are pure. Look for opportunities to be devious in the name of increasing the joy of your group members. Put a piece of bubblegum in their lunch box, tape a cartoon on the ceiling, give everyone a Hershey's kiss as they enter the gym. Do something *really* devious (as long as you're laughing *with* them). Fill a room with balloons or Nerf balls and create some "planned spontaneity." Stay open to play possibilities all around you.

The third one is even less well-known...

Six Great Lines, Cheap Tricks, and Emergency Actions That May Evoke a Smile in Tight Situations

You know, sometimes you're just not perfect or things don't go exactly as planned (e.g., everyone runs away before you say go) or something happens that requires a quick and arbitrary decision to keep the energy going. This is an opportunity for playing with the unexpected. A good leader should always be able to laugh at himself or herself and go with the playful or unexpected moment. Try these lines or actions:

- "Never do this or try this in your home—I'm a professional."

- "I wasn't ready." (Teach them to use this in case they also might not be perfect.)

- "That was just a test." If it had been an actual game...

- "Time-Out—Take Two" (like in the movies).

- "Do over" (e.g., too much wind, too little wind, didn't have the right sunglasses).

- For resolving dilemmas:

  - ask the group ("What do you think?")

  - flip a coin (or spin an executive decision-making spinner)

  - close your eyes, spin around, and point at one of the players to resolve it

  - vote with your body (everyone who thinks this, move over here; everyone else over here)

  - do a quick round of Rock, Paper, Scissors. Whoever "wins" makes the decision

- "That was a practice round. Now it's for realsies."

- "I'll bet someone in this group has a good variation or follow-up game."

- Take the "I don't have to be perfect" pledge (repeat after me). "Repeat after me" pledges can be used very effectively to reinforce safety, fair play, and other principles.

See also Seven Cheap Tricks to Spark Enthusiasm in Chapter 2, *The Fundamentals of Play Leadership*.

All The Equipment You'll Never Need

We're always asked what kinds of equipment we recommend. Our usual response is, "Nothing." The human imagination is the most powerful toy we have (and doesn't need batteries except in John's case), and in our culture we tend to rely too much on gadgets and high-cost purchases to amuse us.

Having said that, some equipment can be nice, and for some groups equipment games are a good familiar "handle" to start off with. Still, you don't have to spend megabucks. In fact, some of our favorite pieces of equipment are recycled (old lengths of jump rope, empty two-liter soda bottles [used in pin guard or as boundaries or as bowling pins], plastic butter tub tops [Frisbees], old bicycle tires used for hoops pass, cutout Clorox bottles for catchers). And we never have to worry about this equipment being damaged!

The other equipment and "toys" that are the best are those that have existed almost forever. These have what games inventor Frank Armbruster called a "figure of elegance." He implied that a good game, toy or piece of equipment should have a simplicity about it (easily handled and learned, simple rules) and multiple uses or strategic possibilities (flexible challenges). That is why balls, blocks, chess, and Scrabble have lasted so long. That is why when we suggest equipment it mostly meets these criteria. In addition to maximum flexibility, we want equipment that is lightweight, soft (for safety) and communicates fun. In Chapter 12, *Resources, Connections, and Beyond*, we'll list a few sources for equipment.

In the meantime, every now and again people ask us what we personally might carry in a...

Minibag

(8-by-8-inch bag with a drawstring)

- 8-inch or larger balloons (can't have too many)

- small beach balls

- small bounceable Nerf balls

- roll of masking tape

- kazoos, sirens, train whistles (other horns, noisemakers)

- mini-Frisbees or flippy flyers

- Magic Markers

- small Guac ball (six-inch, soft, inflatable, bouncing ball)

- various other props (e.g., nose masks, nose whistles, finger puppets, funny buttons you can wear, clown noses)

- 50 feet of thin macramé cord or twine

- colored chalk

- deck of cards

- dice

- small change (pennies, nickels, dimes)

- paper balls

- javaloons (long, inflatable javelin-like balloons)

- bandannas (reds and blues)

Day Pack

(in addition to all of the items in a minibag)

- a few bigger Nerf balls

- Frisbees (a few different sizes)

- wider variety of deflatable balls (e.g., beach balls, Gertie balls)

- foxtails

- more cord (100 feet) or hoopie (or climbing) rope

- old bicycle inner tubes and/or 8- to 10-foot round rope circles (8- to 10-feet of rope with the ends tied together)

- more props
- soap bubbles
- 25- to 50-foot length of clothesline
- ooglic
- face paints and brush(es)
- miniboard games
- funny and/or functional hats
- foam and/or Nerf Frisbees
- a dozen or so bandannas
- old pairs of socks
- old knee socks
- 4-foot lengths of closed-cell foam pipe insulation (make great light portable boffers or taggers)

Duffel Bag

(in addition to all of the items in a day pack)
- boffers (soft foam swords)
- more props
- 2-liter soda bottles with tops (you can fill with water or sand to weigh them down)
- minicones and/or colored spot markers for boundaries
- hoopie rope boundaries
- detachable Hula-Hoops (8 pieces) and/or more rope circles
- sheets or roll of chart paper
- 24- to 30-foot parachute
- playground balls
- more of every kind of ball
- extra mesh equipment bags

- walking boards (cooperative skis) and/or stilts (heavy)

- more Frisbees

- a portable spider web with PVC pipe framework (optional)

Again, the key principles being communicated here with each of the three bags and their contents are lightness (how much do you want to carry), access (the equipment can be used by a wide range of people), softness, maximum flexibility, "big funness," and invitation (come play!).

We encourage you to call AAHPERD, NRPA, or other organizations and get their vendor lists and to get on their mailing lists. You should also haunt garage sales, flea markets, thrift shops, and toy shops. You never know what variety of equipment and props you'll find.

Chapter 10

How to Get Better

Practice, practice, practice!

—The answer to the question, "How do you get to Carnegie Hall?"

Kaizen

Japanese noun—continuous incremental improvement.

Ninja doesn't practice climbing ropes, Ninja climbs ropes!

—unknown Ninja Sensei

Getting better at being a games leader is simple, though it's not always easy. One friend, Dr. Vic Chaissen, from Michigan, said it initially took him about 30 sessions before he was confident going into a group that a game session would work. It may take you more or less time, but the process for improving is the same.

First of all, check your attitude. Make sure you go into every session with good intentions for the players and yourself. Remember, you're a good person. If you weren't, you probably wouldn't be doing this in the first place. If you're a good person, reasonably intelligent (we can't overemphasize this quality), and you like to have fun, then you have what it takes to be a good games leader. Now you have to practice.

The best way to practice leading games is to lead games. So do it. The Japanese have a term, *kaizen,* which means continuous incremental improvement. If you keep an attitude of *kaizen,* looking at every game and session you lead as an opportunity for continuous learning, then you'll find yourself becoming an excellent leader. Here are some suggestions for adding order to your practice and to make your learning as efficient as possible:

Set a Pattern for Learning

Preview it. Do it! Review it. Remember the four Ps from Chapter 3, *Getting It Going*: purpose, planning, preparation, and presentation. Purpose, planning, and preparation are all part of your preview phase. Also, make notes to yourself on any specific areas you want to work on. Then just *do it!* Make your presentation, maintain Flow and Fun, and facilitate a solid closure.

Set Up a Review Pattern

Ongoing evaluation is critical to continued professional development. After each session, take time to review. What happened? What did you do? What worked? What are areas for improvement? What were problem areas where you feel like you could use encouragement and coaching? What do you need to do for follow up? Even 10 or 15 minutes at the end of each session will pay big dividends in the future. One slight course correction now will often make the difference between success and failure in a future program. Don't be too hard on yourself, but also avoid blaming the players (except as a very last resort). While it may sometimes be true that the group was in a bad mood and no matter what you did may not have been successful, most often that is not the case. And blaming "the kids" allows you not to thoroughly analyze all the other factors of your leadership, such as the situation and the setting, that might have been modified to lead to success.

You can develop your own review format to suit your needs, in the same way you might develop an evaluation form for a program. Our suggestion is that you Keep It Splendidly Simple. (Make your system easy to use so you aren't tempted to skip it.)

There are really three basic questions to ask:

1. *What worked?* (aka, Pluses). What were the high points of the session, the Flow Zones? What led up to them? Why did the things that worked work? What did you do that contributed to success? Was it something you said or did in your presentation to maintain the Flow? Are there things which you want to make sure you keep doing in the future or do more of in the future?

2. *What didn't work?* (aka, Minuses or Areas for Improvement). In one way, what didn't work is the good news, since the areas where we are weak are our greatest opportunities for improvement. Understanding what didn't work, and why, will allow you to prepare for the future. In the calm waters after the rapids, take a deep breath, be kind to yourself, and take a few moments to brainstorm alternative routes you might have taken that would not have led to the "dump" (or perhaps a smoother route through the rocky rapids). If you are stuck for ideas about how you might have handled something differently, try contacting a mentor or other more experienced leaders and ask them about alternative approaches. If you have multiple options in your bag of tricks it's likely that one or a combination of them will work.

3. ***What do I want to do in the future?*** The wisdom of hindsight is always clearer. Take advantage of it. Turn the hindsight of each program into foresight for future programs. Make a list of improvements for the future. Remember, every pitfall you avoid and every moment of brilliance you add will increase the Flow for you and the participants.

Keep a "Book"

Earlier we spoke about how baseball teams keep a book on opposing teams and players. They take very explicit notes on the strengths, weaknesses and preferences of the various players. You can do the same quite simply with a loose-leaf notebook and some divider tabs. After each session, add your preview and review notes to your book. You may want to keep it chronological or organize it by type of groups or situations. To this day we both write notes on our "lesson cards" after making a presentation (including the date, size of group, and length of time for each session).

Having your notes in one place will make your planning much easier and faster on future events. You may even develop standardized programs or segments that you can use over and over (because the groups or other profile criteria are similar). You may also want to develop a list of games and reminder notes or a section with bright ideas for possible future use.

Develop Resources

One handy section of your book is a list of resources. Your resource list may be comprised of people, books, facilities, materials, and suppliers. You can use Chapter 12, *Resources, Connections and Beyond*, of this book as a start for your own resource section.

Plan Your Own Development Program

In addition to making sure that you learn from your own experience, take some time out to make sure that you learn from others' experiences as well. Plan your own development program around books to read, games to try, people to meet, mentors to observe and work with, seminars to attend, and even movies and shows to watch. They don't all have to be directly in the area of games or leadership. A seminar on conflict resolution or a psychology book on child development might be very helpful. Eventually everything you know becomes integrated into your leadership, and the more you know the better off you are.

There is no mystery about becoming a *great* games leader. It takes time, practice, persistence, and most of all, will. If you have the will to take the time to learn from your mistakes and from your triumphs, and the persistence to keep learning, you'll do great.

Chapter 11

On the Importance of Being a Playmaker

Better to light a single candle than to curse the darkness.

—Eleanor Roosevelt

The world has its share of misery and woe—there is no doubt about that. Wars, poverty, disease, racism, and the whole gamut of ills have plagued us throughout our history. There often seems to be little that we can do to improve these situations. But we can make a significant contribution by being a playmaker. Through our playmaking skills we *do* make the world better by making life more playful and more joyful for our friends and clients (as well as creating and sharing all the other benefits of play listed in Chapter 1, *On Playing on Purpose*).

Who are the playmakers? They might be anyone who brings the positive power of play and humor to the rest of us. It might be a boss, business manager, or police officer (there is an officer in San Francisco who uses a puppet and his ability to "throw" his voice as a way to educate folks and playfully encourage lawfulness on his beat). It might be a professional comedian or a politician (although they are usually entertaining for other reasons). More often the day-in-day-out playmakers in our society are teachers, recreators, coaches, and childcare and youth workers. Often they are underpaid and undervalued.

The playmaker role is crucial to society, particularly if playmakers are proud advocates of the importance of their contributions. Playmakers can be the joy bringers of society especially for many who have so little joy in their lives. Bringing fun into people's lives provides one of the essential ingredients for healthy individuals and for communities. Beyond the moments of fun that add happiness to people's lives, playmakers provide an important building block for positive values of society. The games we play and the way we play them have the potential to emphasize fairness, personal and team accomplishment, responsibility, celebrating diversity, and meeting challenges— all critical to personal success and to the success of our society. As a role model as well as a service deliverer, playmakers can go beyond being entertainers or caretakers to truly being teachers in the greatest sense of the word.

If we as playmakers consciously and conscientiously choose to make full value of our work, we can make a great contribution to society. We can help bridge the rifts in society by turning the metaphorical "playground" into a common ground where diverse people can come together and create community through the common spirit of play. The experience of play is universal.

It crosses boundaries of age, race, sex, culture, and time. Throughout history people have played and we can guess that many of the feelings of healthy play in the past (even if the materials differed), were the same as they are now. Through play, we can create a safe space for all different types of people to meet, have fun, enjoy each other's company, get to know one another, and potentially to become friends. In any day and age, especially ours, creating fun, trust, and friendship is a powerful accomplishment.

For each individual who has a chance to play, we're offering a doorway to well-being. Many books have been written on the role of laughter and play in healing. As playmakers, each time we help someone achieve a state of playfulness we're contributing to his or her wellness. As we help groups play together, we're contributing to society's wellness.

In many spiritual philosophies from around the world a person's journey through life is referred to as a *path*. Those of us who are playmakers have chosen to walk the Playful Path. To successfully walk this path and reach its further destinations, we need to have the same discipline as a martial artist, a warrior, a monk or a doctor. We need to study and learn the cognitive knowledge of games, of people and of play. We need to practice with discipline, to gain the skills physically, emotionally, and verbally, to lead play with others and nurture it within ourselves. We need to practice our art in the same way that people sincerely practice their religion or doctors sincerely practice medicine. We need to contemplate and reflect on *what* we're doing, as well as the *whys* and *hows* of our actions. Through our contemplation we can help keep ourselves centered on the ethics and values of the Playful Path which are most important to convey.

Above all, we need to practice being open to learn new ways to play, to recognize the playfulness of others, and to nurture improving the quality and the quantity of our own playfulness. This is what makes for a challenging practice, continually looking inward and outward.

Imagine, if there were a giant fun game and everyone in the world was playing. Not just participating mind you, but in the Flow, in the spirit of true play, for the joy and fun of all the participants. None of this distortion of play like unethical competition, overcommercialization, or cheating. We are all playing fully, for the fun of it. If we could accomplish this, we would certainly have made the world a better place. Each of us has the potential as a playmaker to throw a stone in the pond and add many ripples of positive interaction.

Maybe the one world game is a little much to expect, but we can work in that direction. The easiest and the hardest place to start is with ourselves. Practicing to see the play and joy in life, even when it doesn't seem playful. Learning to play with our own frailties and to laugh at ourselves is not always easy. Practicing being the playmaker that we want to be and modeling for other people takes a great deal of discipline. To share a level of play that is sacred and profound and fun is a great accomplishment. To do that will require changing ourselves and making ourselves better playmakers and better people. If we achieve that we'll have made the world a more positive peaceful playful place.

Imagine...

—John Lennon

Chapter 12

Resources, Connections, and Beyond (The Bigger Picture)

Play is the exaltation of the possible.
—Martin Buber

Throughout this book we've done our best to share with you our years of experience with play facilitation to help you become a better play leader. We hope that in addition to the techniques and principles in the book an overriding message that comes across is the importance of attention to *P* words. Not only planning, preparation, presentation, pasta, pizza, and peanut butter, but also the big three: *process, people,* and *playfulness.*

Beyond Games

The games or activities we share are merely a tool or vehicle to serve people's needs. The spirit of playfulness is bigger than and transcends any activity, and what is most important is to lead those activities in a way that facilitates individual and collective growth, development, self-esteem and *fun.* In other words we as play leaders should be paying attention to our process of play leadership (including the process of group dynamics) so that we assure a playful, healthy, growth-filled atmosphere.

If we have that perspective as a leader and pay attention to *process, people*, and *playfulness* there is no limit to the play possibilities and applications around us, both personally and professionally. With sensitive responsive leadership, games can be powerful tools. Many people might think of games as only a part of traditional recreation, youth development, childcare or physical education programs. While this may be true, we invite you to consider expanding your perspective on how and where games and play experiences might be applied. Over the years we've developed programs and been involved in almost all of the following applications of play and games.

In Business and Organizational Settings

- As team builders, communication and problem-solving metaphors

- To energize a meeting by starting it with a five-minute game

- Company picnics or retreats

- Visualization exercises to envision successful solutions to challenges

- As part of an employee wellness program

- As a specific wellness tool (laughter therapy)

- To build group social support and collective wellness within families, organizations and groups

- For stress reduction, for diversion, arousal, relationship building, and positive mind–body connection

- The power of laughter, humor, and play in the workplace (holistic play–work merger)

- For successful aging programs

- For natural alternatives to drug use and abuse

In Schools and Children's Centers

- As rainy day, between subject fillers

- Combined with "academics" to motivate and reinforce subject matter

- For fun, physical fitness activities

- As a self-esteem and/or leadership development program

- As a multicultural and/or mainstreaming integration tool

- As an energy changer or diverter (to quiet down or energize)

- As a leveler or icebreaker for parents, teachers and students (back-to-school nights, PTA activities)

For Friends and Families

- As a family home evening activity games night (alternative to media)

- Around the dinner table

- As a way to playfulize the house (game chests, dice dishes, cleanup wheel, refrigerator magnet letters)

- Family festivals, celebrations, and parties

- On trips

As a Community Organizing Tool

- For meetings (so people will at least come for the "serious" issues)

- In church groups to affirm values (e.g., family, togetherness, joy)

- For neighborhood block parties and to "reclaim" parks for all the residents of a community (not just the drug dealers)

As a Creativity Exercise or Exercise in Self-Renewal

- Having a games invention–games variations workshop.

- Suppose we modified some of our favorite games and played them in different environments (e.g., in the snow, in a swimming pool, in the dark with glow sticks) or with different movements or equipment. Think about tick-tack-toe or Electronic Battleship.

- Suppose we just wanted to noodle around without having to be good at something (the creative exploratory process).

- Suppose we want to use play to open ourselves up to creativity (whole brain–right brain), integrative, multiple intelligence ways of learning.

Miscellaneous

How many more can you think of?

- In camps

- In lines at Disneyland

- In airports

- As a way to develop positive caring behaviors or assist with conflict resolution (in childcare centers, schools)

- On wilderness trips

An Even Bigger Picture

If we come back to our premise that games are merely tools and the most important thing is your facilitation, then another even bigger picture emerges. That is, how can you (or anyone else as a teacher–leader) take the facilitation techniques and principles of this book and apply them to other situations and settings that are not necessarily "play centered"? We strongly believe that much of what is in the book has broad-based applications. But that is another book altogether. Allow us, however, to give you a few examples:

- In business and organizational management, the concepts of empowerment and facilitative leadership are crucial. So are ways to successfully motivate, recognize, and energize your workers.

- In developing special events (whether they be corporate or community events or a child's birthday party) all of the principles of planning, preparation, and how to get people involved and have fun are relevant.

- Successful classroom teaching certainly incorporates everything from attention getters to a successful merger of fun and focus.

- Creative arts and environmental education activities leaders can certainly utilize the techniques of motivation, organization, and the facilitation of psychological safety.

- Coaches who want to keep sports healthy and keep winning in perspective can certainly utilize team-building facilitation techniques, fun developmental drills, and a maximum participation–motivation approach when working with their players.

- People interested in developing creativity in the populations they work with can utilize ways to open up the group process so it's safe to explore and to express oneself, and to integrate and warm up both hemispheres of the brain.

Thus the games and play leadership techniques and principles in this book take on a broader meaning of sensitive humanistic leadership in whatever settings or situation we may find ourselves. Paying attention to the following becomes important wherever we are and it doesn't matter whether we are leading a game or arts and crafts or coaching a sport, teaching a class, running a meeting, or sitting around the family dinner table:

- Keep it interactive and involving.

- Keep it fun, challenging and motivating.

- Create "safety zones" and "permissions" for people to try, to risk, to express themselves, to create, to not be perfect.

- Empower people and be responsive to their needs.

- Pay attention to process and group dynamics.

- Practice flexibility (in planning and implementation) and changing the "game" when it isn't working.

As leaders, if we can implement these, we go a long way toward making a better world.

Resources

Thousands of books and periodicals relate to games (e.g., games involving math, party games, travel games, games for insomniacs) and we've owned and used hundreds of them in our 30 years of play leadership. We will not attempt to list these but highlight (and annotate where appropriate) a limited selection of books that we've found most useful (and gone back to again and again). If you're looking for a particular area of games or play resources feel free to call us and for only a small fortune and the pink slip to your car we'll research it and give you our best suggestions and recommendations. You'll also find that most of our carefully thought out suggestions will have massive bibliographies of other books and resources. Also, particularly pay attention to the catalogs and organizations listed in this section. Get on their mailing lists—this will open up even more resource possibilities. We especially urge you to call the toll-free 800 numbers, explore the websites, and order the catalogs. Almost all of them are *free* and packed with excellent books, equipment, and other resources. We have attempted to be *very* selective. You won't be disappointed. And, of course, access keywords on the World Wide Web for even more resources.

In addition, we also suggest haunting old bookstores, flea markets, garage sales, thrift shops, discount stores, teacher supply stores, party stores, and your local library (look under games, sports, hobbies, simulations, play, recreation, amusements, children, and fun). We find some of our best resources in these places. And don't neglect old games books. Remember games are a form of folklore and they often come back around in a different or recycled form. An old game may trigger a new twist or variation. For example, as mentioned earlier, variations of the presently popular board game Pictionary are found in old parlor games books that are over 100 years old!

We think the resources listed here are *hot!* If you have other resources, books, catalogs, or videos that you believe should be considered for the next edition of this book please let us know. We are bound to have offended someone with our sins of omission (but we don't feel that guilty).

Catalogs, Magazines, and Newsletters

American Alliance for Health, Physical Education, Recreation, and Dance (AAHPERD)
1900 Association Drive, Reston, VA 20191-1598
phone 703-476-3400 or 800-213-7193
http://www.aahperd.org

American Association for the Child's Right to Play
Rhonda Clements, Graduate Physical Education
240 Hofstra University, Hempstead, NY 11548
phone 516-463-5176; fax 516-463-4810
http://www.ipausa.org
(child-centered play resource)

American Camping Association
5000 State Road 67 North, Martinville, IN 46151
phone 765-342-8456; fax 765-342-2065
http://www.acacamps.org
(good collection of adventure, leadership, environmental education and activity resources)

Animal Town
P.O. Box 757, Greenland, NH 03840
phone 800-445-8642

The Association for the Study of Play
c/o A. M. Guilmette Ph.D.
Dept. of Recreation and Leisure Studies
Brock University, St. Catherine's, Ontario L25 3A1, Canada
phone 905-688-5550, ext. 3124; fax 905-688-0541
(play theory and applications)

BSN Sports
P.O. Box 7726, Dallas, TX 75209
phone 800-527-7510; fax 800-899-0149
http://www.bsnsports.com
(one of many equipment companies)

Canadian Council on Children and Youth
323 Chapel Street, Ottawa, Canada K1N 7Z2
(various play/leadership/training resources)

Committee for Children
568 First Avenue South, Suite 600, Seattle, WA 98104-2804
phone 206-343-1223 or 800-634-4449; fax 206-438-6765
http://www.cfchildren.org
(good conflict resolution materials)

Educators for Social Responsibility
Resources and Training for Empowering Children Catalog
23 Garden Street, Cambridge, MA 02138
phone 617-492-1764; fax 617-864-5164
http://www.esrnational.org
*(a valuable resource connecting books and other resources on conflict reso-
lution with cooperative play, initiative games, and problem solving including*
Adventures in Peacemaking—A Conflict Resolution Guide for School-Age
Programs. *Get this!)*

ERIC Clearing House on Rural Education and Small Schools
Appalachia Educational Laboratory
P.O. Box 1348, Charleston, WV 25325-1348
phone 304-347-0428 or 800-624-9120; fax 304-347-0467
http://www.ael.org/eric
(good adventure, environmental and experiential education resource)

ERIC Clearing House on Teaching and Teacher Education
One Dupont Circle, Suite 610, Washington, DC 20036
phone 800-822-9229

Games Publications Inc.
Games Magazine
P.O. Box 203, Marion, OH 43305-0203
phone 800-426-3768

Human Kinetics
P.O. Box 5076, Champaign, IL 61825-5076
phone 800-747-4457
http://www.humankinetics.com
(good activity and elementary physical education resources)

The Humor Project
480 Broadway, Suite 210, Saratoga Springs, NY 12866-2288
phone 518-587-8770
http://www.humorproject.com
(outstanding collection of team-building, creativity, games, humor and heal-
ing resources. Get this!)

International Association for the Child's Right to Play (IPA)
http://www.ipaworld.org
PlayRights (newsletter)
    Brian J. Ashley, Editor
    Ludvigsbergsgatan 10
    S-118 23 Stockholm, Sweden
    phone Int. + 46 + (0)8-669 75 68
    e-mail brian.ashley@telia.com
Alternate Contact
    IPA Play Resources
    3 Earnings Street, Godmanchester, Huntingdon, Cambridge PE 18 8JD,
    England
    phone Int. + 44 + (0)1480 441 384; fax Int. + 44 + (0)1480 386 510
Alternate Contact
    Professor Robin Moore
    P.O. Box 7701 School of Design
    North Carolina State University, Raleigh, NC 27695-7701
    phone 919-821-4913; 919-515-8344; fax 919-834-8446
Alternate Contact
    Monty Christiansen
    1155 Smithfield Street, State College, PA 16801-6429
    phone 814-238-2160; fax 814-861-2261
    e-mail montyc@psu.edu

Kendall/Hunt Publishing Co.
4050 Westmark Drive, P.O. Box 1840, Dubuque, IA 52004-1840
phone 563-589-1000 or 800-228-0810; fax 563-589-1046 or 800-772-9165
http://www.kendallhunt.com
(perhaps the best adventure/experiential education resource. It includes
Project Adventure resources, teamwork, and environmental games, and ac-
tivities. Order this!)

Klutz Press
455 Portage Avenue, Palo Alto, CA 94306
phone 800-737-4123
http://www.klutz.com

Learned Enterprises International, Inc.
W9115 Bluewaters Pass, Cambridge, WI 53523
phone 608-423-9779 or 800-462-0411; fax 608-423-3535
http://www.experientialeducator.com

National Recreation and Parks Association
22377 Belmont Ridge Road, Ashburn, VA 20148
phone 703-858-0784
http://www.nrpa.org

Oriental Trading Company, Inc.
Box 2308, Omaha, NE 68103-0407
phone 800-875-8480
http://www.oriental.com
(miscellaneous and sundry inexpensive fun stuff, props, and toys)

Pfeiffer and Company
2780 Circleport Drive, Erlinger, KY 41018
phone 800-272-4434
(one of many good teamwork and organizational development resources. A good place to start!)

Project Adventure, Inc.
701 Cabot Street, Beverly, MA 01915
phone 978-524-4500; fax 978-524-4501
http://www.pa.org
(one of the best collections of adventure, problem-solving, initiative activities and leadership approaches. Get it!)

Redleaf Press
450 North Syndicate, Suite 5, St. Paul, MN 55104
phone 651-641-0305 or 800-423-8309; fax 651-645-0990 or 800-641-0115
http://www.redleafpress.org

School-Age Notes
After School Program Resource Catalog and *Newsletter for School-Age Care Professionals*
P.O. Box 40205, Nashville, TN 37204-0205
phone 615-279-0700 or 800-410-8780; fax 615-279-0800
http://www.schoolagenotes.com
(comprehensive and accessible activity and leadership resources including the best positive discipline books)

Venture Publishing, Inc.
Books That Matter (catalog)
1999 Cato Avenue, State College, PA 16801-3238
phone 814-234-4561; fax 814-234-1651
http://www.venturepublish.com
(very good activity and leadership resources)

YMCA Member Store
c/o Crown Prince, Inc.
5695 West Franklin Drive, Franklin, WI 53132
phone 877-742-5686; fax 414-421-3970
http://www.ymca.net

Zondevan Publishing House
5300 Patterson Avenue Southeast, Grand Rapids, MI 49530
phone 800-934-6381
(good classic game books for family and older youth groups, especially those by Rice, Rydberg and Yaconelli)

Books, Videos, Journals, and Magazine Articles

We've significantly limited this list to books, magazine articles, and videos we've used (some of which are now classics), liked, borrowed (and returned), or know enough about to recommend them (but we couldn't buy them all because we would have gone broke). The marvelous thing is that since the publication of *New Games* and *More New Games* 20-plus years ago there has been a proliferation of excellent books and other sources that emphasize joyful, cooperative play, initiative and adventure activities, and competitive games with creative inclusive modifications. We've also included a few articles that more specifically expand on several topics we mention in the book (e.g., discipline alternatives, theoretical issues, and applications). We hope you'll find these useful. Send us suggestions for updates in the next edition. Also in our opinion, the classics listed here are still very useful (that's why they are classics—older is sometimes better—just like us).

Baldwin, B. (1985). *It's all in your head: Lifestyle management strategies for busy people.* Wilmington, NC: Direction Dynamics.
(one of the best explications of the connections between stress, guilt and play, with many practical, playful healing strategies for healthy individuals and families)
Belitz, C. and Lundstrom, M. (1997). *The power of flow.* New York, NY: Harmony Books.
(practical ways to transform your life using flow theory)
Cain, J. and Joliff, B. (1998). *Teamwork and teamplay.* Dubuque, IA: Kendell Hunt.
(comprehensive teambuilding and leadership processing resource)
California Department of Education. (1994). *Kids Time: A School-Age Care Program Guide.* California Department of Education Publication Sales Units, P.O. Box 271, Sacramento, CA 95812-0721; phone 916-445-1260; fax 916-323-0823.
(excellent concise practical guide to program leadership and behavioral management)
Canadian Council on Children and Youth. (1978). *Play Leadership Training I and II.* 323 Chapel Street, Ottawa, Ontario, Canada K1N 7Z2.
(a strong collection of training the trainer materials)
Canadian Parks and Recreation Association. (1984). *Fitnic: A Community Festival of Fitness, Fun, Food, Friends, Family.* Canadian Parks and Recreation Association, 333 River Road, Vanier, Ontario, Canada K1L 8H9.
(still perhaps the best, most accessible laymen's guide to organizing a large or small play event—great checklists and timelines)

Cooper, A. (1998). *Playing in the zone—Exploring the spiritual dimensions of sports.* Boston, MA: Shambhala Publications.
(a good concise summary of flow and play and other higher consciousness connections to play, games, and sport)

Cornell, J. (1998). *Sharing nature with children.* Nevada City, CA: Dawn Publications.
(the classic in its area—the best place to start for nature, and ecological games and activities)

Csikszentmihalyi, M. (1997). *Finding flow: The psychology of engagement with everyday life.* New York, NY: Basic Books.
(quality of life and happiness connections of Flow work, play and leisure)

Csikszentmihalyi, M. (1990). *Flow: The psychology of optimal experience.* New York, NY: Harper and Row.
(one of the theoretical foundations of quality play leadership and quality lives)

Davis, R. (1991). *Totally useless skills—101 pastimes of practically no redeeming value.* New York, NY: Perigree.
(amazing, amusing—add to your nonmarketable skills while nurturing the player in you and adding to your presentation repertoire)

De Koven, B. (1978). *The well-played game—A players philosophy.* Garden City, NY: Anchor/Doubleday.
(the classic explication of win–win play by one of the founders of the New Games movement. Required reading!)

Devney, D. (1990). *Organizing special events and conferences.* Sarasota, FL: Pineapple Press Inc.
(a practical guide for busy volunteers and staff)

Ferrell, T. and Eisenberg, L. (1975). *Sneaky feats—The art of showing off and 53 ways to do it.* New York, NY: Sheed and Ward, Inc.
(more ways to nurture your foolishness and amuse your friends)

Fink, D. (1995). *Discipline in school-age care: Control the climate not the children.* Nashville, TN: School Age Notes.
(a concise, practical approach to positive discipline)

Fluegelman, A. and The New Games Foundation (Eds.). (1976). *The new games book.* Garden City, NY: Dolphin/Doubleday.
(this is what started the ongoing "new play," collaborative, creative, adventure, laughter, humor, team-building movements. A still valuable classic filled with great games and sixties retrospectives!)

Fluegelman, A. and the New Games Foundation (Eds.). (1981). *More new games.* Garden City, NY: Dolphin/Doubleday.
(a follow-up collection of great games, leadership suggestions, and the invent-a-game guide; both new games books have been heavily borrowed from by subsequent games, play, adventure and training books)

Gregson, B. (1982). *The incredible indoor games book.* Carthage, IL: Fearon
Teaching Aids.
(good collection)

Gregson, B. (1984). *The outrageous outdoor games book.* Carthage, IL:
Fearon Teacher Aids.
(another good collection)

Gregson, B. (1991). *Take part art—Collaborative art projects.* Carthage, IL:
Fearon Teacher Aids.
(an original new gamester artist—great book on cooperative art projects)

Jackson, R. (1997). *Making special events fit in the 21st century.* Champaign,
IL: Sagamore Publishing.
(very practical diverse advice and event ideas from a master)

Jackson, R. and Schmacher, S. (1997). *Special events inside and out.*
Champaign, IL: Sagamore Publishing.
(a "how to" approach to event productions marketing and sponsorship)

Johnson, D. and Johnson, F. (1997). *Joining together: Group theory and
group skills.* Needham Heights, MA: Allyn & Bacon.
*(the most comprehensive, usable book on group skills, group dynamics
and leadership. A must for leaders!)*

Jones, R. (1989). *The unusual world records book.* Ron Jones Publishing,
1201 Stanyan Street, San Francisco, CA 94117.
*(a marvelous collection of collaborative, creative, playful challenges in
the new games spirit for special populations and all of us)*

Kirk, D. (1990). Peace table. *School Age Notes, 11*(2), 5.
(good explanation of an excellent conflict resolution alternative)

Krane, G. (1998). *Simple fun for busy people—333 free ways to enjoy your
loved ones more in the time you have.* Berkeley, CA: Conari Press.
*(a nice collection of play possibilities in everyday life; e.g., in lines, at
work, at meals, with chores)*

Kreidler, W. and Furlong, L. (1995). *Adventures in peacemaking—A conflict
resolution guide for school-age programs.* Cambridge, MA: Educators
for Social Responsibility/Project Adventure.
*(outstanding resource using cooperative activities, valuing communica-
tion, and conflict resolution strategies to create peace on the playground,
in the classroom and in the world).*

Lawyer-Tarr, S. (1999). Time for "time out" to retire—Let "balance center"
take its place. *School Age Notes, 19*(8), 1, 3.
(an expanded description of a time-out alternative)

Michaelis, B. (1977). *Learning through noncompetitive activities and play.*
Pacifica, CA: Children Together.
(one of the updated "originals"—a fine collection of cooperative/creative

games and movement activities for the munchkins [pre-Kindergarten through third grade]). Order from Children Together (see organizations)

Michaelis, B. (1977, Summer). Flow/New games. *New Games Foundation Newsletter,* 1, 2.
(the original flow-play connection article)

Michaelis, B. (1978, Winter). Creating the playful space...It power...A game detergent. *New Games Foundation Newsletter,* 4, 5.
(an expansion on the it power–flow connection)

Michaelis, B. (1984). The family that plays together...Programming, marketing and delivering family play ideas. *California Parks and Recreation Magazine,* 4(1), 38–41.
(a wide range of family play applications)

Michaelis, B. (1988). Child's play under siege. *School Age Notes,* 9(1), 1, 2.
(current negative impacts on childhood and children's play and what to do about them)

Michaelis, B. (1990). *Facilitating Playfulness and Cooperative Interaction: Principles of Leadership and the Development of Psychological Safety* (video). Order from Leisure Learning Laboratories, San Francisco State University, Department of Recreation and Leisure Studies, San Francisco, CA 94132.
(excellent interactive leadership training video)

Michaelis, B. (1990). *The fundamentals of play leadership: New games/adventure games.* Pacifica, CA: Children Together.
(a good collection of can't miss games for all age groups and group sizes plus sections on leadership, applications, team-building, discipline and conflict resolution). Order from Children Together (see organizations)

Michaelis, B. (1990, Spring). A common sense approach to discipline: Active positive assertive leadership. *California School Age Consortium Review,* 4(2), 2, 3.
(more on discipline and effective communication with kids)

Michaelis, B. (1991). Fantasy, play, creativity and mental health. In T. Goodale and P. Witt (Eds.), *Recreation and leisure: Issues in an era of change* (3rd ed.; pp. 55–72). State College, PA: Venture Publishing, Inc.
(a good explication of play theory and related issues)

Michaelis, B. (1991). The case for cooperative play. *Play Rights—IPA Journal,* 12(4); 13(1), 1–4.
(a good expanded argument for collaborative activities)

Michaelis, B. (1997). *How to Lead Games* (video). Pacifica, CA: Children Together.
(outstanding leadership video that complements this book—a wide variety of can't miss games, leadership hints, attention getters and team di-

viders; ways to promote physical and psychological safety and ideas for modifying activities). Order from Children Together (see organizations) or BillandEzra.com.

Michaelis, B. (2001). *The Best Frisbee and Balloon Games for Older School-Age Kids, Teens, Adults, and Families* (video). Pacifica, CA: Children Together.
(Frisbee baseball, guts Frisbee, pro-am partner Frisbee golf, water balloon volleyball surprise, balloon basketball, no-base baseball, and much more. More than twenty great games and variations for groups of 2–200. Includes written rules, creative leadership hints, safety tips, and follow-up resources. 38 minutes. This is a very hot video! Created and led by Dr. Bill.). Order from Children Together (see organizations) or BillandEzra.com.

Michaelis, B. and Holland, E. (2003). *The Best Cooperative Team Building Activities for all Ages and Organization* (video). Pacifica, CA: Children Together.
Catch the energy of this fast paced engaging video designed for both the novice and the experienced group leader or corporate trainer and the widest range of ages and abilities. Over 20 of our favorites (Arrows, Down Under, Tarp Turnover, Euro Traffic Circle, Powerful Partners, Pacific Pipeline, Closing Circles and much more). Plus countless variations of each activity allowing for a selective balance of challenge, focus and fun; Processing and leadership hints, written rules and a modeled sequence of group building from start to finish. (58 minutes) Led by Bill and Ezra. Order from Children Together (see organizations) or BillandEzra.com.

Michaelis, B. and O'Connell, J. (1987, Winter). Family leisure education: A model, some strategies and program development case studies. *California Parks and Recreation Magazine, 43*(1), 20–23.
(more family play applications)

Michaelis, B. and Therrell, J. (1997). *Fun, Fast and Easy—A Players Dozen of the Best Activities to Play With School-Age Children—With Leadership Tips* (video). Austin, TX: Play Today.
(great games filmed with kids—comes with 14 detailed activity descriptions and variations). Order from Children Together (see organizations)

Mitchell, J. (1996). *Home sweeter home: Creating a haven of simplicity and spirit.* Hillsboro, OR: Beyond Words Publishing Inc.
(a beautiful, practical, spiritual guide to creating playful, loving, caring families)

Moore, A. (1992). *The game finder—A leaders guide to great activities.* State College, PA: Venture Publishing, Inc.
(a good accessible collection)

Morton, A., Prosser, A., and Spangler, S. (1991). *Great special events and activities.* State College, PA: Venture Publishing, Inc.
(a collection of unique special events and "how to" suggestions)

Nachmanovitch, S. (1990). *Free play—Improvisation in life and art.* Los Angeles, CA: Jeremy Teacher, Inc.
(a highly readable book, the best ever written on the connections between play and creativity—another quality of life classic)

Niepoth, W. (1983). *Leisure leadership.* Englewood Cliffs, NJ: Prentice Hall.
(a very good synthesis of leadership processes, group skills and interpersonal relationships)

Orlick, T. (1978). *The cooperative sports and games book.* New York, NY: Pantheon/Random House.
(the original cooperative sports and games book. Also check out Orlick's follow-up book and his newest offering, Feeling Great). Order through Kendall/Hunt.

Orlick, T. (1982). *The second cooperative sports and games book.* New York, NY: Pantheon/Random House.
(the follow-up book still packed with great ideas)

Rice, W., Rydberg, D., and Yanconelli, M. (1977). *Fun and games—A source book of games for the whole family.* Grand Rapids, MI: Zondervan.
(still one of the most accessible comprehensive games books, with great sections on water games, special events, "wide" games [like capture the flag] and others that other books don't have)

Rohnke, K. (1984). *Silver bullets.* Hamilton, MA, Project Adventure, Inc.
(the original classic adventure games book by the "godfather" of the adventure movement; be sure to also check out the latest resources [The Bottomless Bag Again?!, Funn Stuff, Quicksilver, Top Tricks, and others])

Scannell, E. and Newstrom, J. (1997). *The complete games trainers play on CD-ROM.* New York, NY: McGraw Hill.
(CD-ROM version of the Games Trainers Play *series by the same authors. Useful reworkings of new games, icebreakers, and problem-solving activities for organizational settings)*

Sutton Smith, B. and Sutton Smith, S. (1974). *How to play with your children (and when not to).* New York, NY: Hawthorne Books. *(one of the most practical, readable explications of the developmental stages of play, birth through teens, and what we can do about them)*

Therrell, J. (1988). *How to play with kids.* Pfleugerville, TX: Play Today Press.
(a good usable resource from one of Bill's former graduate students who has done fine work on his own)

Therrell, J. (1997). *The Essentials of Play Leadership* (video). Pfleugerville, TX: Play Today Press.
(basic play leadership illustrated with kids)

Weinstein, M. and Goodman, J. (1980). *Playfair.* San Luis Obispo, CA: Impact Publishers.
(Matt and Joel were there early on and have continued to do progressive work/play in the corporate/humor/team-building areas)
Westland, C. and Knight, J. (1982). *Playing, living, learning: A worldwide perspective on children's opportunities to play.* State College, PA: Venture Publishing, Inc.
(a book of 186 of the most progressive children's play programs around the world)

~~Organizations~~ *izations and Networks*

In this section we have included a selective listing of organizations and networks that are solid sources of information and resource people related to the topics in this book. The best approach is to contact them and request publications and general information about the organization, conferences, etc., and to get on their mailing lists if possible. We'd especially like to put in an extra plug for the Humor Project (see Catalogs, Magazines and Newsletters), Project Adventure (see Catalogs, Magazines and Newsletters), The Association for Experiential Education, The International Association for the Child's Right to Play (see Catalogs, Magazines and Newsletters), Children Together, and InterPlay Network. Again, forgive our sins of omission and send us your suggestions for additional worthy groups and resources for inclusion next time.

American Society for Training and Development
1640 King Street, Box 1443, Alexandria, VA 22313-2043
phone 703-683-8100 or 800-628-2783; fax 703-683-8103
http://www.astd.org
(one of the best most comprehensive sources for information on people, seminars, and books related to training and development. They also have regional affiliated groups around the country)

Association for Applied and Therapeutic Humor
1951 W. Camelback, Suite 445, Phoenix, AZ 85015
phone 602-995-1454; fax 602-995-1449
http://www.aath.org
(a wide range of articles, materials and conferences related to creative applications of fun, play, laughter and humor)

The Association for Experiential Education
2305 Canyon Boulevard, Suite 100, Boulder, CO 80302-5651
phone 303-440-8844; fax 303-440-9581
http://www.aee.org
(excellent organization of diverse experiential educators. Resources include journal, newsletter, publications, conferences and affiliate groups in training and development, and therapeutic adventure. Great source of people and materials related to adventure and collaborative play)

BillandEzra.com
(Bill Michaelis and Ezra Holland's brand new website detailing training and event services, products and resources for the widest range of topics and clientele. Serious Fun)

California School-Age Consortium
657 Mission Street, Suite 601, San Francisco, CA 94105
phone 415-957-9775; fax 415-957-9776
(pioneering national work in diverse school-age training)

Cal Poly Annual Elementary Physical Education Workshop
c/o California Association of Health, Physical Education, Recreation, and Dance
1501 El Camino Avenue, Suite 3, Sacramento, CA 95815-2742
phone 916-922-3596 or 800-499-3596
http://www.epew-cp.com
(one of the best "hands on" creative games play and sport conferences lead by leading practitioners—practical, positive kid stuff)

The Children's Television Resource and Education Center
444 DeHaro, Suite 202, San Francisco, CA 94107-2347
phone 415-864-8424
(publishes various prosocial behavior resources, including the Getting Along After School Project—*a collection of art, games, science, nature, and activities promoting cooperation and conflict resolution)*

Children Together—An International Play Event and Leadership Training Organization
Bill Michaelis, Ph.D., Director and Professor
San Francisco State University
338 Reichling Avenue, Pacifica, CA 94044
phone 650-359-0836 or 415-338-7576; fax 650-359-0841; e-mail wiljmich@sfsu.edu
(an excellent source of games, play, leadership, conflict resolution, staff development and team-building workshops, events, keynotes, books, and videos since 1974. Call or write for free brochure and information packet, including order forms, expanded keynote and workshop descriptions, and excellent references from around the world)

Experiential Educator
phone: (800) 462-0411; fax (608) 423-3535
http://www.experientialeducator.com/
(an incredible source of activity and training information and products by good hearted people who know how...)

www.fishphilosophy.com
Chart House International Learning Corporation
221 River Ridge Circle, Burnsville, MN 55337
phone 800-328-3789; fax 952-890-0505
*(a great source of books and products about creating fun and a positive work
atmosphere in organizations)*

Happy Productions Inc.
1208 Cardinal Court, Altamonte Springs, FL 32714
phone 407-296-2058; fax (same)
http//members.aol.com/gethappy13
*(Jim Atkinson and his happy cohorts are doing some fine work in the games
and play leadership area—good workshops and resource books)*

Interplay Network Inc.
John O'Connell, Director
15 7th Avenue, San Francisco, CA 94118
phone 415-386-3528; fax 415-386-6887
*(an excellent source of workshops and events on play leadership, team-build-
ing and organization development since 1979 with the widest range of corporate and public clients)*

National Association for the Education for Young Children (NAEYC)
1509 16th Street, NW, Washington, D.C. 20036-1426
phone 202-232-8777 or 800-424-2460; fax 202-328-1846
http://www.naeyc.org
*(a good source of Early Childhood Education play books and materials espe-
cially for younger children)*

National School-Age Care Alliance
1137 Washington Street, Dorchester, MA 02124
phone 617-298-5012; fax 617-298-5022
http://www.nsaca.org
*(this organization is doing very progressive training in games, play, conflict
resolution, and other activities)*

New Games
P.O. Box 1641, Mendocino, CA 95460
phone 707-962-0514
http://www.newgames.com

The Outdoor Network—The Global Forum for Outdoor Professionals
P.O. Box 1928, Boulder, CO 80306-1928
phone 303-444-7117; fax 303-447-8322
http://www.outdoornetwork.com
(comprehensive network of outdoor resources including training, team building, adventure games, conferences, and ropes courses and extensive newsletters)

Padagogische Aktion/Spielkultur
Augustenstrasse 47/Rgb, München, Germany
phone 089/2609208, fax 089/268575, e-mail spielkultur@pask.muc.kobis.de
http://www.pa-spielkultur.de
(although there are many fine international play organizations (best identified through IPA and/ or individual country representatives or through Westland), this group is one of the best, most creative, progressive, long lasting play and culture organizations in the world and well-respected and connected in the world play community. They have published scores of books, done huge events, conducted international conferences on theoretical and applied play, created a children's museum and many other programs (especially merging the cultural arts, high-tech and high-touch play)—a model organization of what can and needs to be done)

Playfair, Inc.
2207 Oregon Street, Berkeley, CA 94705
phone 510-540-8768 or 800-750-5439; fax 510-540-7638
http://www.playfair.com
(one of the original alternative play organizations still successfully doing corporate and organizational events, and workshops)

Play for Peace
4750 North Sheridan Road, Suite 225, Chicago, IL 60640
phone 773-275-0077; fax 773-275-3385
www.playforpeace.org
(international initiatives, events and workshops using creative collaborative play to promote peace)

...ly Inc.—Peak Potential Through Positive Play
Faith Evans, Director
348 Driftwood Circle, Lafayette, CO 80026-3151
phone 303-664-5374; fax 303-664-5375
(workshops and other resources. Faith is one of the best pure-hearted play facilitators in any universe)

Play Today
c/o Jim Therrell
17315 Manish Drive, Pflugerville, TX 78660
phone 800-359-7331
(training, books, videos, other materials. Jim is one of Bill's former graduate students who has done very well with his national play leadership organization)

Project PLAE/MIG Communications
800 Hearst Avenue, Berkeley, CA 94710
phone 510-845-7523; fax 510-845-8750
(play and learning in adaptive environments—very good materials and workshops on play safety and creative play environments that integrate people of different abilities; also award winning communication/design consultants)

Radworks
43617 Buckeye Terrace, Fremont, CA 94538
phone 888-478-CAMP
http://www.jonessquare.com/camprena
(a growing resource network of good play books and videos including Bill's How To Lead Games *(which can also be ordered through him at Children Together)*

Sharing Nature Foundation/Sharing Nature Worldwide
14618 Tyler Foote Road, Nevada City, CA 95959
phone/fax 530-478-7650
http://www.sharingnature.com
(a wealth of excellent nature and ecological games and resources)

Teamtime Trainings
Alois Hechenberger
Amthorstrasse 5, A-6020 Innsbruck, Austria
phone: 43(0) 699/100 64 774; fax: 43(0) 699/400 64 774
e-mail: a.hechenberger@teamtime.net
http://www.teamtime.net
(great international play training and leadership resources)

Teamwork and Teamplay
468 Salmon Creek Road, Brockport, NY 14420-9761
phone 585-637-0328; fax 585-637-5227
http://www.teamworkandteamplay.com
(a very good source of training, books, materials, organizations, resources and a comprehensive annotative bibliography in the book Teamwork and Teamplay *by Cain and Joliff)*

Further Services and Sources of Information From Us

We would love to work and/or play with you! Contact Bill through Children Together or BillandEzra.com and John through Interplay Network, Inc.

Closings

> *He was born with the gift of laughter and the sense that the world was mad.*
> —Santayana

We hope that we've excited you about the possibilities of play and play leadership. As Martin Buber wrote many years ago, "Play is the exaltation of the possible." If we stay open to playfulness and continue to nurture our inner child-player-imagination, the possibilities are endless. To play with anything, everything or nothing with anyone, everyone, anywhere—this is our joyful challenge. It's possible...

Tag you're it—Have fun!

(.gninnigeb eht si sihT)

About the Authors

Bill Michaelis is Professor, former Graduate Coordinator, and former Chair of the Department of Recreation and Leisure Studies at San Francisco State University. He is the director of Children Together, an international play event and leadership training organization. Over the past 25 years Bill has presented over 1,500 fun-filled, thought-provoking workshops, events, and keynote speeches around the world to clientele as diverse as Paramount Pictures and the government of Austria. He has presented keynote addresses at annual association conferences in 17 different states and workshops for many more. He has presented to just about every type of organization that serves children and youth, including schools, human service and recreation organizations, nonprofit, public and corporate childcare agencies, and the widest range of professional conferences. His extensive event work includes a 10,000-person family play festival in the Olympic Park in Munich, Germany.

He has written, taught, and consulted extensively in the area of play and its applications to creativity, learning development, self-esteem, and healthy living for all age groups. He was a lead trainer and board member of the original New Games Foundation. He is the author of "Fantasy Play Creativity and Mental Health" and *Learning Through Noncompetitive Play Activities,* and was a contributor to *The New Games Book* and *More New Games* (which he also coedited.) He has also recently produced three excellent training videos on play and games leadership.

Bill received both his master's and doctoral degrees in Education and Anthropology from the University of California at Berkeley, emphasizing Play and Human Development and Multicultural Education. He currently lives in Pacifica, California, with his wife Dinah, and his two grown "kids" Paige and Jason are still close by in the Bay area.

John O'Connell is director of Interplay Network, an organization development firm specializing in process facilitation, leadership, team development and conflict resolution. He has worked with a wide range of organizations across the country, from AT&T to The Nature Conservancy. He has also worked across many levels and boundaries within organizations from union members to the top management team at Chrysler Corporation.

John was codirector of the New Games Foundation and lead developer of the New Games Training Program. He was a contributing author of *The New Games Book.* John is particularly well-known for his work in "active learning," using learning games, sea kayaking, and exercises drawn from the martial art of Aikido as methods for experiential education. He integrates the range of his work experience through a variety of methodologies to engage a group or an organization in the "organizational learning" process. John currently lives in San Francisco with his wife Susan Haldeman, an attorney mediator, and their son Terrence Morgan.

Collectively, Bill and John have worked with at least half a million people, conducting thousands of games and play leadership workshops, conference programs, presentations, classes and events throughout the United States, in Canada and in Europe. Together they have written articles and consulted extensively in the area of play and games as they apply to personal, community and organizational development. Over the past 25 years, the authors have helped develop and promote the "facilitative leadership" approach, which is now being popularized in the business world as the "new leadership" paradigm. They have been at the forefront of applying this approach in the recreation and education fields.

Bill can be reached at Children Together and BillandEzra.com. John can be reached at Interplay Network Inc.

Index

Other Books by Venture Publishing

The A•B•Cs of Behavior Change: Skills for Working With Behavior Problems in Nursing Homes
by Margaret D. Cohn, Michael A. Smyer, and Ann L. Horgas

Activity Experiences and Programming within Long-Term Care
by Ted Tedrick and Elaine R. Green

The Activity Gourmet
by Peggy Powers

Advanced Concepts for Geriatric Nursing Assistants
by Carolyn A. McDonald

Adventure Programming
edited by John C. Miles and Simon Priest

Assessment: The Cornerstone of Activity Programs
by Ruth Perschbacher

Behavior Modification in Therapeutic Recreation: An Introductory Manual
by John Datillo and William D. Murphy

Benefits of Leisure
edited by B. L. Driver, Perry J. Brown, and George L. Peterson

Benefits of Recreation Research Update
by Judy M. Sefton and W. Kerry Mummery

Beyond Baskets and Beads: Activities for Older Adults With Functional Impairments
by Mary Hart, Karen Primm, and Kathy Cranisky

Beyond Bingo: Innovative Programs for the New Senior
by Sal Arrigo, Jr., Ann Lewis, and Hank Mattimore

Beyond Bingo 2: More Innovative Programs for the New Senior
by Sal Arrigo, Jr.

Both Gains and Gaps: Feminist Perspectives on Women's Leisure
by Karla Henderson, M. Deborah Bialeschki, Susan M. Shaw, and Valeria J. Freysinger

Client Assessment in Therapeutic Recreation Services
by Norma J. Stumbo

Client Outcomes in Therapeutic Recreation Services
by Norma J. Stumbo

Conceptual Foundations for Therapeutic Recreation
edited by David R. Austin, John Dattilo, and Bryan P. McCormick

Dimensions of Choice: A Qualitative Approach to Recreation, Parks, and Leisure Research
by Karla A. Henderson

Dementia Care Programming: An Identity-Focused Approach
By Rosemary Dunne

Diversity and the Recreation Profession: Organizational Perspectives
edited by Maria T. Allison and Ingrid E. Schneider

Effective Management in Therapeutic Recreation Service
by Gerald S. O'Morrow and Marcia Jean Carter

Evaluating Leisure Services: Making Enlightened Decisions, Second Edition
by Karla A. Henderson and M. Deborah Bialeschki

Everything From A to Y: The Zest Is up to You! Older Adult Activities for Every Day of the Year
by Nancy R. Cheshire and Martha L. Kenney

Protocols for Recreation Therapy Programs
edited by Jill Kelland, along with the Recreation Therapy Staff at Alberta Hospital Edmonton

Quality Management: Applications for Therapeutic Recreation
edited by Bob Riley

A Recovery Workbook: The Road Back from Substance Abuse
by April K. Neal and Michael J. Taleff

Recreation and Leisure: Issues in an Era of Change, Third Edition
edited by Thomas Goodale and Peter A. Witt

Recreation Economic Decisions: Comparing Benefits and Costs, Second Edition
by John B. Loomis and Richard G. Walsh

Recreation for Older Adults: Individual and Group Activities
by Judith A. Elliott and Jerold E. Elliott

Recreation Programming and Activities for Older Adults
by Jerold E. Elliott and Judith A. Sorg-Elliott

Reference Manual for Writing Rehabilitation Therapy Treatment Plans
by Penny Hogberg and Mary Johnson

Research in Therapeutic Recreation: Concepts and Methods
edited by Marjorie J. Malkin and Christine Z. Howe

Simple Expressions: Creative and Therapeutic Arts for the Elderly in Long-Term Care Facilities
by Vicki Parsons

A Social History of Leisure Since 1600
by Gary Cross

A Social Psychology of Leisure
by Roger C. Mannell and Douglas A. Kleiber

Special Events and Festivals: How to Organize, Plan, and Implement
by Angie Prosser and Ashli Rutledge

*Steps to Successful Programming: A Student Handbook to Accompany Programming for
    Parks, Recreation, and Leisure Services*
by Donald G. DeGraaf, Debra J. Jordan, and Kathy H. DeGraaf

Stretch Your Mind and Body: Tai Chi as an Adaptive Activity
by Duane A. Crider and William R. Klinger

Therapeutic Activity Intervention with the Elderly: Foundations and Practices
by Barbara A. Hawkins, Marti E. May, and Nancy Brattain Rogers

Therapeutic Recreation and the Nature of Disabilities
by Kenneth E. Mobily and Richard D. MacNeil

Therapeutic Recreation: Cases and Exercises, Second Edition
by Barbara C. Wilhite and M. Jean Keller

Therapeutic Recreation in Health Promotion and Rehabilitation
by John Shank and Catherine Coyle

Therapeutic Recreation in the Nursing Home
by Linda Buettner and Shelley L. Martin

Therapeutic Recreation Protocol for Treatment of Substance Addictions
by Rozanne W. Faulkner

Tourism and Society: A Guide to Problems and Issues
by Robert W. Wyllie

*A Training Manual for Americans with Disabilities Act Compliance in Parks and Recreation
    Settings*
by Carol Stensrud